ALL OR NOTHING

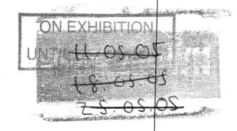

ALL OR NOTHING
Mike Leigh

faber and faber

First published in 2002
by Faber and Faber Limited
3 Queen Square London WC1N 3AU
Published in the United States by Faber and Faber Inc.
an affiliate of Farrar, Straus and Giroux LLC, New York

Typeset by Country Setting, Kingsdown, Kent CT14 8ES
Printed in England by Mackays of Chatham plc, Chatham, Kent

© Mike Leigh 2002

The right of Mike Leigh to be identified as authors of this work
has been asserted in accordance with Section 77
of the Copyright, Designs and Patents Act 1988

A CIP record for this book
is available from the British Library

ISBN 0-571-21687-0

2 4 6 8 10 9 7 5 3 1

CAST AND CREW

All Or Nothing was first shown on 17 May 2002 at the Cannes Film Festival. A Les Films Alain Sarde/Thin Man Films production, produced by Alain Sarde for Studio Canal.

MAIN CAST
(*in order of appearance*)

RACHEL	Alison Garland
OLD LADY	Jean Ainslie
PHIL	Timothy Spall
PASSENGERS	Badi Uzzaman
	Parvez Qadir
NUTTER	Russell Mabey
PENNY	Lesley Manville
MAUREEN	Ruth Sheen
SMALL BOYS	Thomas Brown-Lowe
	Oliver Golding
	Henri McCarthy
	Ben Wattley
RON	Paul Jesson
NEVILLE	Gary McDonald
DINAH	Diveen Henry
YOUNG MAN	Leo Bill
MAN WITH FLOWERS	Peter Stockbridge
GARAGE OWNER	Brian Bovell
RORY	James Corden
SAMANTHA	Sally Hawkins
CRAIG	Ben Crompton
CAROL	Marion Bailey
DONNA	Helen Coker
JASON	Daniel Mays
SID	Sam Kelly
HAROLD	Timothy Bateson
CARE WORKER	Michele Austin
NEUROTIC WOMAN	Alex Kelly
DRUNK	Allan Williams
MC	Peter Yardley
SINGER	Dawn Davis

PARTY-GIRLS	Emma Lowndes
	Maxine Peake
MEN AT BAR	Matt Bardock
	Mark Benton
SILENT PASSENGERS	Dorothy Atkinson
	Heather Crancy
	Martin Savage
FARE DODGER	Joe Tucker.
MARTHA	Edna Doré
CÉCILE	Kathryn Hunter
ANGE	Georgia Fitch
MICHELL	Tracey O'Flaherty
SUPERVISOR	Di Botcher
NURSE	Valerie Hunkins
DOCTOR	Robert Wilfort
CRASH DRIVER	Daniel Ryan

MAIN CREW

Written and Directed by	Mike Leigh
Produced by	Simon Channing Williams
Cinematographer	Dick Pope
Editor	Lesley Walker
Music	Andrew Dickson
Production. Designer	Eve Stewart
Costume Designer	Jacqueline Durran
Make-Up and Hair Designer	Christine Blundell
Sound Recordist	Malcolm Hirst
Line Producer	Georgina Lowe
Casting	Nina Gold

All Or Nothing

Titles over . . .

A long, empty institutional corridor with a shiny floor. Patches of bright sunlight.

A large young woman wearing an apron moves into view. She is mopping the floor, working her way from side to side. She is Rachel.

A very old lady in a dressing gown appears at the far end of the corridor. She moves slowly towards Rachel, supporting herself on the handrail and with a stick. This place is clearly a care home for elderly people.

Rachel carries on. She rinses out the mop in a bucket. Then she stops to let the old lady pass.

RACHEL

Be careful – the floor's wet.

The old lady ignores her.

D'you wanna 'and?

Rachel goes to help her, but the old lady shrugs her off, and moves away. Rachel watches her go for a few moments. Then she resumes her work.

In a moving saloon car, in a busy sunlit urban street. Two men are sitting in the back seat. The older man clutches some battered luggage. They are talking in Punjabi, though the English words 'restaurant' and 'illegal' can be discerned. The driver says nothing.

Now a grubby young man in biker's gear swigs from a can of lager in the back seat of the same car. It will become apparent that he is something of a Nutter. The car has the same driver, Phil. He is slightly dishevelled – stubble, longish hair, open-neck shirt, old leather jacket, a worried air.

PHIL

D'you break down?

NUTTER

What?

PHIL

D'you 'ave an accident?

NUTTER

No . . . some fuckin' monkey cunt nicked my bike, man!

He punches the front seat violently.

Fuckin' cunt!! Fuckin' cunt!! Fuckin' cunt!!

Phil looks alarmed.

A large, busy supermarket. Two women cashiers sit back-to-back at their checkout posts, processing shopping. Penny is facing us. Maureen has her back to us. Both wear spectacles. Maureen turns round.

> MAUREEN
> 'Ere, Pen, fancy goin' out?

> PENNY
> When?

> MAUREEN
> Saturday?

> PENNY
> Er . . . Yeah . . . alright, then.

> MAUREEN
> (*jokey*)
> Oh, don't be so enthusiastic!

We hold on Penny as she continues to work. She has a tired, pinched, weary look.

Phil's car again – obviously a mini-cab. His back-seat passengers are now a jostling, squabbling gang of small boys in posh grey school caps and blazers. Phil speaks into a walkie-talkie.

PHIL

One-three.

A woman controller replies over the air.

CONTROLLER

Yeah?

PHIL

I'm clearing Cranston Road in a minute or two.

In the mini-cab office. The controller is Dinah, late twenties.

DINAH

Can you just wait?

She sits behind a security grille, watched by a bald man in a suit. He stands behind her, smoking a fag. This is Neville, her brother and the boss. Dinah writes something, then passes a bit of paper through the grille to a waiting driver, who takes it and leaves.

The driver is Ron, mid-fifties, well built, remains of 1960s long hair, moustache and sideburns, also smoking a fag. He carries a newspaper under his arm.

Outside, we see him leave (a shop: 'Gladiator Cars').

Back inside.

DINAH

Can you pick up at 12 Bellott Street, SE10, going to Charlton?

PHIL
(*over noisy kids*)

Say again.

DINAH

12 Bellott Street, yeah?

PHIL

Going to Charlton – got it.

Ron in his car, parked outside a small terrace house. A lanky young man closes the front door and scuttles towards the car.

RON

Mr Eyles?

YOUNG MAN

Yeah – er, Elephant and Castle.

He gets in the back, and closes the door. Ron moves off, and starts a three-point turn. But he backs into a concrete bollard, which is situated on the pavement. There is a distinct crunch.

RON
(*inside*)

Awgh! Oh, Christ . . .

He gets out. He is wearing his shades. The Young Man gets out, too. They survey the damage together for a moment.

I don't fuckin' believe it!!

A few minutes later. Ron is sitting in his stationary car, still wearing his shades. He is speaking into his walkie-talkie.

RON

Listen, I've got to get the car fixed – some bitch in a Volvo's smacked me up the arse. I've got no fuckin' lights.

In the mini-cab office. Neville responds. He is standing. Dinah sits by the phone, next to him. She is filing her nails.

NEVILLE

Ron, I told you – no swearin' over the air. What's goin' on?

RON

I gotta get the car off the road.

NEVILLE

Why, what's the damage?

In Phil's car. Phil and his back-seat passenger, an elderly gentleman holding a bunch of flowers, overhear the conversation between Ron and Neville . . .

RON

She's buggered me tail-lights – I ain't legal!

NEVILLE

Is the car mobile?

RON

Driveable, yeah . . .

NEVILLE

Well, just come back to base.

Dinah is attending to her lips.

RON

I can't do that, Neville.

NEVILLE

Come back to base, and get it done tomorrow.

RON

No – I gotta do it now!

NEVILLE

Listen, Ron, don't mess me about – I'm short of drivers.

8

Dinah is now leafing through a clothing catalogue.

RON

Neville: fuck off!!

He turns off his walkie-talkie.

This conversation hangs in the air in Phil's car, as he and his elderly passenger continue their journey in silence. Phil glances in his mirror.

Now, in an empty suburban cemetery, the elderly gentleman walks up a long path between the gravestones. Phil leans on his car and watches him thoughtfully from a distance.

At a crash-repair garage. Ron and the Garage Owner stand at the rear of the damaged car. Ron smokes a fag.

RON

'Ow much?

OWNER

Overnight?

Ron nods.

'Undred and fifty. (*He sips a cup of tea.*)

> RON

Best you can do?

> OWNER

You wannit in the mornin', innit?

He shrugs, and bends down to examine the damage more closely. Phil pulls up in his car.

> RON

'Ello, Phil.

> PHIL

Hello, Ron.

> RON

Got smacked up the arse.

> PHIL

Yeah – heard it on the radio.

The Garage Owner is pulling broken bits of plastic out of the tail-light.

Are you leavin' it 'ere?

> RON

Yeah.

> PHIL

Well . . . I'll run you 'ome.

> RON

Oh, cheers, mate.

The supermarket staff entrance. Maureen emerges into the bright sunlight, followed by Penny. They come down a busy flight of steps. Each carries shopping in a Safeways bag. Neither is wearing spectacles.

> MAUREEN

Innit nice?

PENNY

Yeah.

MAUREEN

Feel like sun-bathin'. Get me bikini on. Not! I'll see you later . . . alligator!

PENNY

T'ra, then.

They go off in opposite directions.

A busy main road. Penny is on her bicycle. Her shopping is in the front basket, and she is wearing a rucksack and a crash helmet.

A bus stop. Lots of people and traffic. Maureen sits, waiting. The bus arrives. She stands up, gets out her ticket, and boards it.

Penny cycles across a barren piece of ground in the middle of a bleak, grey concrete housing estate. She passes a large young man who is kicking a football against a wall.

PENNY

'Ello, Rory.

RORY

Alright?

PENNY

You alright, Craig?

Craig, another young guy, dishevelled and grubby, is watching Rory. So is a young woman, Samantha, who is wearing chopped-off jeans. Rory is wearing a T-shirt and tracksuit bottoms.

SAMANTHA
(*as Penny passes her*)

Yeah, alright?

PENNY
(*timidly*)

Yeah . . .

She gets off her bike, and proceeds to walk up a ramp. As she passes Samantha again . . . .

Comin' in for your tea, Rory? About twenty minutes . . .

RORY

Alright.

Craig kicks the ball. Rory grabs him, thumps him on the back, and throws him to the ground.

Fuck off, Craig!! Fuckin' wanker!!

Penny quickly parks her bike and runs back towards the boys.

PENNY

Rory! What're you playin' at?!

Rory passes her, going the other way.

RORY

'Es always doin' that!!

PENNY
(*to Craig*)

Are you alright?

Craig nods.

Did 'e 'urt yer?

CRAIG

Nah.

Penny hovers for a moment, then leaves Craig, who shouts to Rory:

'T's only a ball!!

Penny joins Rory at a graffiti-covered lift.

PENNY

What're you doin'?

RORY

'E's a tosser.

PENNY

'E ain't a tosser.

The lift door opens. More graffiti inside. Rory enters. Penny follows with her bike.

You're not at school now, you know.

RORY

I know!

PENNY

What time d'you get up this mornin'?

RORY

I dunno!

PENNY

Yes, you do; what time d'you get up? (*She presses the button.*)

RORY
(*overlapping*)

No, I don't – I dunno!

PENNY

Probably about two o'clock, I expect.

The lift door closes.

Moments later, Penny follows Rory along their sixth-floor walkway balcony. Glimpse of rooftops, another high-rise, etc.

PENNY

You should leave 'im alone, Rory, 'e's smaller than you!

RORY

So? 'E's older.

PENNY

Yeah, but you're bigger.

RORY

Why are you takin' 'is side, Mum?

PENNY

I ain't takin' 'is side.

RORY

Yes, you fuckin' are!

PENNY

Don't swear.

Rory pounds on a front door. Penny stops, and takes off her rucksack. Rory gives the door another clump.

Yeah, it's alright – I've got me key.

She gets out her key. Rory knocks yet again, aggressively.

RORY

Come on!!

PENNY

Don't shout.

RORY

What's she doin'?!

PENNY

I dunno – she's probably on the toilet or something!

She puts the key in the lock. At this moment the door is opened from the inside by Rachel, who was mopping in the first scene. As the door opens, Rory barges in.

Rory!!

RORY
(*to Rachel*)
What's wrong with you?

PENNY
What's wrong with you, you mean! (*She wheels her bike into the flat.*) Alright?

RACHEL
Yeah. I'm alright. (*She closes the door. A sad look in her eyes.*)

A few minutes later, in the small kitchen. Penny takes a bottle of cola out of the fridge, and pours herself a glassful. Rachel fills a kettle and plugs it in.

PENNY
What've you been doin'?

RACHEL
Nothing. Just readin'.

She gets a mug and prepares a hot drink.

PENNY
'Ow's work?

RACHEL
Alright.

PENNY
Everyone okay?

RACHEL
Yeah . . .

She takes the lid off a large biscuit tin. Penny leans against the sink and sips her drink.

What's for tea?

PENNY
Chicken and vegetable pies.

RACHEL
D'you wanna biscuit?

PENNY

No.

Rachel takes a bite of biscuit.

In an empty pub. Phil and Ron sit side by side with their backs to the window, mostly silhouetted against the early-evening summer light. Both take swigs from pint glasses of lager. Ron smokes a fag.

PHIL

You alright, mate?

RON

Yeah.

PHIL

You ain't got no whiplash, nor nothing?

Short pause.

RON

She fucked off.

PHIL

Did she?

RON

Mm.

PHIL

D'you exchange insurance details with 'er, 'n' that?

RON

I pulls over . . . (*He grunts, meaning 'understood?'*) She scarpers.

PHIL

That's not very nice, is it?

RON
(*disgusted*)

Fuckin' women.

PHIL

Wouldn't be a world without 'em, mate. (*He sips his beer.*) Anyway, she might've done you a favour.

RON

'Ow d'yer mean?

PHIL

Well . . . if it adn't've 'appened, you might've driven round the next corner and killed a little kid. 'S wotsit, innit? – fickle finger of fate. I mean, if you knew what was goin' to 'appen to you when you woke up in the morning, you'd never get out o' bed. That's life . . . the old clock ticks; world turns round, tide comes in, tide goes out. You're born, you die. That's it. (*He takes another sip of beer.*)

RON

What's your missus make at Safeway?

PHIL

I dunno, to tell you the truth.

RON

What, you dunno what she earns?

Enough, huh. Keeps the wolf from the door. With the bit
I make.

*Penny's grey, concrete housing estate, another part of it. Maureen
arrives on foot, carrying her shopping. She climbs a shabby exterior
staircase. She obviously lives here, too.*

*Phil and Ron have just got out of Phil's car, which he now locks. As
they walk together, it becomes clear that we are yet again on this same
housing estate. Ron is smoking a fag, and Phil carries some packages.
A man passes them, carrying a spade and a carrier bag. Phil and Ron
come across Samantha and Craig, who are hanging around some
steps. Phil and Ron stop.*

SAMANTHA

Alright?

PHIL

'Ello.

*Pause. Then Ron moves off. Phil joins him, and they walk across a
baldish patch of dry grass. Now they are in the spot where Penny
earlier met Rory and the others.*

RON

I'll see you tomorrow.

PHIL

Yeah – see you, Ron.

*They part. Ron wanders away, across the estate. A few people come
and go, including a man with a dog. As Phil disappears into his
building, the camera tilts up it, floor by floor. A young woman hurries
along one of the walkways. Phil enters his flat and closes the front
door. He goes to the kitchen, where Penny and Rachel are cooking.*

PHIL

Alright?

RACHEL

Alright?

PENNY

What you got there, then?

PHIL

Burger buns. Three dozen.

PENNY

Well, we ain't gonna eat all them.

PHIL

No, it's alright – they're long-life . . . look . . .

PENNY

What's the expiry date?

PHIL

Er . . . twenty-fourth of October.

PENNY

That's – that's four months away.

PHIL

Yeah.

PENNY

Cor – what they got in 'em, then?

PHIL

I dunno. (*He puts them down.*) Chemicals. Picked a bloke
up from the cash-'n'-carry. 'S trying to get a refund on 'em,
they wouldn't ave it. (*He chortles.*) 'E give 'em to me as a
tip. 'E was drunk. 'E bought 'em for a barbecue . . . and no
one turned up.

PENNY

We'll 'ave to get some burgers, then.

PHIL

Yeah.

*The sound of gunshots on the television draws Phil's attention to Rory,
who is lying on the sofa in the living room. Phil ambles towards him as
Penny starts to set the table.*

Alright, boy? What you been up to today, then? (*He takes off
his jacket.*)

PENNY

'E's been fightin' today.

PHIL

What?

RORY

Fuck off, Mum!

PENNY

Rory, will you stop swearin' at me, please?

PHIL

You been clumpin' people again?

RORY

Don't listen to 'er – she don't know nothin' about it.

PENNY

'S 'cos 'e ain't got nothing to do with 'imself.

RORY

Shu' up, 'e was askin' for it.

PENNY

'E's mopin' about 'ere all day, lookin' for trouble.

RORY

(*sitting up*)

I ain't lookin' for trouble – I ain't done nothin'!

PENNY

When are you gonna take 'im up the Job Centre?

RORY

Fuck's sake, I'll get a job when I want, it ain't got nothin'
to do wi' you – just stop goin' on about it!!

PENNY

Rory, calm down – nobody's 'avin' a go at yer, I'm just
tryin' to 'elp yer.

Gunshots on the TV.

RORY

Fuck off!

*Penny looks expectantly at Phil, but he says nothing, and moves away
to hang up his coat in the hall.*

*A little later. They are all sitting round the table, eating a knife-and-
fork meal. Rory has his plate on his knees, and is watching a TV
programme in which an audience is laughing uproariously at
something. He is half-turned away from the others. Penny looks
anxious.*

PHIL

Filled the car up with petrol this morning. Thirty-eight
quid.

Pause.

Been busy?

PENNY

Yeah. Rory, can you put your plate on the table, please?

Yeah, alright!!

He puts his plate down aggressively. Pause. More mirth on the TV.

PHIL

Picked up a doctor's surgery, dinner time. Old bloke . . . 'e 'ad one o'them, er . . . wossername, frames . . .

RACHEL

Zimmer.

PHIL

Yeah. 'E only wanted to go to the next street. I says . . . 'Sorry, mate, I gotta charge you the minimum fare, three pound fifty.'

PENNY

You shouldn'ter charged 'im nothin'!

PHIL

No . . . I know. I said, 'Oh . . . call it a coupla quid.'

PENNY

You shouldn'ter called it nothin'!

PHIL

Well . . . 'e wasn't 'avin' it – 'e insisted on givin' me the full fare.

PENNY

But you didn't 'ave to take it, though, did yer?

PHIL

No . . . but . . . it's, wossername, innit, 'is . . .

RACHEL

Dignity.

PHIL

Yeah. No price on that when you're old. (*TV mirth.*) Ron's 'ad a bump. Some old woman ran into 'im.

PENNY

Is it a write-off?

PHIL

No. I said to 'im, 'Make the most of it, mate. 'Ave the day off.'

PENNY

'E likes workin'. (*She looks towards the window.*) It's a nice evening tonight.

PHIL

Yeah.

PENNY

I ain't been for a walk for ages. (*to Rachel.*) You fancy goin' for a walk later on?

RACHEL

No, not really.

PHIL

Take you out for a drink, if you like.

PENNY

No.

Rory puts down his cutlery with a clatter, and flops onto the sofa.

Rory!

RORY

What?!

PENNY

Well, we ain't finished yet.

RORY

So?

PENNY

There's pudding.

RORY

I know!!

In Maureen's flat. She goes to the foot of her stairs. (All the apartments we see on this estate are situated on two floors and have staircases.

Although they are therefore technically not 'flats' but 'maisonettes', they are usually known as flats, and are thus so called here.)

MAUREEN
(*calling upstairs*)

Are you in, Donna?

DONNA
(*from upstairs*)

Yeah.

MAUREEN

D'you wanna bit o' chicken pie?

DONNA

No!!

Maureen goes into her kitchen.

In Ron's flat. His wife, Carol, in a white dressing gown and with unkempt hair, sits huddled on a sofa. Ron removes some dirty dishes from a cluttered coffee table in front of her.

CAROL

Leave that. I'll do it later . . .

RON

Christ Almighty, you've had all day.

Carol swigs some beer from a pint glass. The TV is on – a rowdy game show. A clatter of dishes from the kitchen; then Ron returns. Carol manoeuvres herself into a comfortable horizontal position, and Ron settles down in his armchair. He has a pint of beer and a fag.

CAROL

D'you wanna go out later?

RON

What?

CAROL

Little drink.

RON

No.

CAROL

Why not?

RON

I've 'ad a rough day.

CAROL
(*uninterested*)

'Ave yer?

Samantha comes in from outside. She puts her bag and keys in the hall, and goes into the living room.

SAMANTHA

What're you doin' for tea, Dad?

RON

I don't know!

SAMANTHA

Can we get a takeaway?

RON

No.

SAMANTHA

Right. Let's all starve, then, shall we?

She goes into the kitchen.

RON

What's in the freezer?

SAMANTHA

Not a lot.

RON

Well, what?

Samantha checks out the freezer.

SAMANTHA

A sausage meal and a raspberry ripple.

She comes back into the living room.

RON

Is that all?

SAMANTHA

Yeah.

CAROL

There's two chicken kormas in there.

SAMANTHA

No, there ain't.

RON

We 'ad them last night.

CAROL

No, we never.

RON

Yes, we did.

SAMANTHA

Yeah – me an' Dad.

RON

You never 'ad nothin'.

SAMANTHA

She never fuckin' does.

Carol struggles with her memory.

So, what are we doin', then?

RON

Oh, maybe I'll get a takeaway.

SAMANTHA

When?

RON

Later.

SAMANTHA

Well, I ain't 'ad nothin' to eat since I got up.

RON

Well, 'oose fault's that?

SAMANTHA

I'm starvin'!

RON

You ain't done nothin' since you got up!

SAMANTHA

Well, what about 'er? Lazy cow.

She refers to Carol, who sips her beer and takes no notice.

RON

When are you goin' to get a job?

SAMANTHA

Fuck off!!

She stomps off upstairs, grabbing her bag from the coat hook in the hall as she goes. A coat falls down, but she doesn't stop to pick it up.

Maureen is in her living room, ironing. She is surrounded by racks of clean skirts, dresses etc. Donna lies on the sofa, smoking a fag.

She wears a tight top, slacks and trainers. The TV is playing the programme Carol has just been watching.

MAUREEN

What's the matter? Ain't you 'ungry again?

DONNA

No, I ain't.

MAUREEN

What, you're on a diet?

DONNA

Nah.

MAUREEN

You look like a skeleton.

DONNA

Shu' up! 'T's better than bein' fat, innit?

MAUREEN

Yeah, it is.

DONNA

Yeah, it is.

MAUREEN

Exactly – so what 're you complainin' about?

DONNA

I ain't complainin'. It's you that's complainin'.

MAUREEN

I ain't complainin' – I like a bit of fat. Keeps me warm at night.

DONNA

'T's all you got to keep you warm at night.

Maureen lets this pass.

MAUREEN

I'll make you some mashed potato.

DONNA

I don't want mashed potato.

MAUREEN

Chips?

DONNA

I'll 'ave a few chips.

MAUREEN

'Ow many's a few?

DONNA

A few!!

MAUREEN

Two?

DONNA

Funny!

MAUREEN

Three?

DONNA

Shu' up!

Maureen is amused.

MAUREEN

Are you goin' out tonight?

DONNA

Yeah.

MAUREEN

Where are you goin'?

DONNA

Out!

MAUREEN

Oh, I've been there!

DONNA

'Ave yer?

MAUREEN

Yeah – it gets a bit packed, though, dunnit?

DONNA

Yeah, it does.

MAUREEN

'Oo're you goin' out with, Scarface?

DONNA

(sitting up)

Shu' up! That's bang out of order, that is!

MAUREEN

D'you want this duvet cover on your bed?

She is folding the duvet cover she has just been ironing.

DONNA

No, I don't! And what are you ironing that for, anyway?
Nobody irons duvet covers.

MAUREEN

I do, if someone pays me for it. I'll iron anything, within
reason. I'll put a few chips on. Two, wunnit?

She goes into the kitchen.

*A bit later on this summer evening. Samantha is leaning on the
balustrade on the walkway outside her third-floor flat. She is looking
down at Craig, who is standing some distance away on the ground
by another building. He is gazing back at her and smoking a fag.
Maureen comes out of the flat immediately next to Samantha's. She
is carrying a few freshly ironed garments on hangers. She closes her
front door.*

MAUREEN

Alright, Sam?

SAMANTHA

Alright?

MAUREEN

You locked out?

SAMANTHA

No.

31

MAUREEN

Oh – good. Is your mum in?

SAMANTHA

Yeah.

Maureen sets off along the walkway. A young man in a bomber jacket strides purposefully across the estate. Samantha shows some interest in this development and moves along the balustrade a little, watching him. A few moments later he passes beneath Maureen, who has now progressed to the first-floor walkway of an adjacent block.

MAUREEN

Evenin', Jason.

JASON
(*without stopping*)

Yeah, alright?

MAUREEN

She's ready for you.

JASON

Is she?

MAUREEN

Only took her two hours.

They part. Maureen goes off with her ironing. Samantha watches Jason disappear into her block. She leans against the balustrade, waiting for him. A few moments later he appears. She watches him come towards her.

SAMANTHA

Alright?

JASON

Alright?

He is aggressive. He sports an earring and a facial scar. He stops at Donna's flat, and knocks on the door.

SAMANTHA

'Ow're you doin'?

JASON

Yeah, not bad.

SAMANTHA

Takin' 'er out, are yer?

JASON

Yeah, o' course.

SAMANTHA

Where're you goin', then?

JASON

Down the pub.

SAMANTHA
(sarcastic)

That's nice.

JASON

Where are you goin'?

SAMANTHA
(saucy)

I dunno.

She smiles at him. He looks at her. A moment takes place. The door opens, and Donna emerges. She is wearing very short shorts.

DONNA

Alright?

JASON

Alright – come on. (*He sets off.*)

SAMANTHA

Alright, Donna?

DONNA
(aggressive)

Yeah.

She follows Jason.

SAMANTHA

Can I come too?

DONNA

No, you can't!

SAMANTHA

Why not?

DONNA

Fuck off!!

Samantha is amused. Then, to herself, drily:

SAMANTHA

'Ave a nice time without me.

Maureen, returning from having delivered her work, passes Donna and Jason on the walkway.

MAUREEN

You off?

DONNA

Yeah.

MAUREEN

Be good. If you can't be good, be careful.

DONNA

Fuck off!

Maureen laughs, and arrives at her flat. She lets herself in. As she does so she glances at Samantha, who ignores her and turns round to watch Donna and Jason. They now appear below, bickering.

SAMANTHA
(*shouting*)

There's no need to argue about it!

DONNA
(*shouting back*)

Shu' up!!

Donna and Jason keep walking.

Alright, Craig?

Jason suddenly lurches aggressively towards Craig.

JASON

Oi, what?!

As he is holding Donna's hand, she is dragged along with him.

What d'you keep fuckin' lookin' at me for? Don't fuckin'
look at me – I'll fuckin' slice you, you cunt!

DONNA

Jase –

JASON

Fuckin' mug! Fuckin' wanker!

*Samantha is much amused by all this. Donna and Jason move away
from Craig. Jason barks at Donna:*

Get your fuckin' 'ands off me!!

*And off they go, bickering their way across the estate. The entertainment
over, Samantha goes indoors, throwing Craig a quick glance over her
shoulder as she does so. Left alone, he continues to gaze up towards her
flat. But he doesn't move.*

*That night. Rory is lying on his tummy on the sofa, watching TV
(a movie: another shoot-out). Phil is working his way along the sofa,
feeling the cushions.*

RORY

What're you doin', Dad? Ge' off!!

PHIL

Come on, shift over.

RORY

What're you lookin' for?

PHIL

Money . . .

RORY

There ain't none down there.

PHIL

Come on, get up.

RORY

I'm tellin' yer: there ain't none –

Phil lifts up the cushion under Rory's head.

Oh, shit!

A coin. Rory grabs it.

PHIL

Here, give us it.

RORY

No, that's mine. (*He puts his weight back on the cushion.*)

PHIL

Come on, give us it – Rory, give us it.

RORY

No – finders keepers.

PHIL

Look, don't mess about.

RORY

No! Fuck off!

PHIL

Look, I'll give you – I'll give you double tomorrow. Come on.

RORY

Nah.

Pause.

PHIL

I ain't joking.

RORY

Well, you can borrow it, but you owe me a quid – alright?

PHIL

Alright.

Rory holds up the coin. Phil tries to take it, but Rory grips it firmly.

Come on – let go.

Rory lets go.

    Ta.

Phil moves away. Rory carries on watching the movie.

Now into his hand Phil empties the contents of a small brass ornament (a miniature tricycle with a bucket between its back wheels). He discards various items (a paper clip, a battery, an eraser, a pen-top, a lozenge), leaving only some coins, which he checks. Then he walks away, with the coins.

He climbs the stairs.

Rachel is in her bedroom, in bed, reading a book. A knock on the door.

RACHEL

    Yeah?

Phil puts his head round the door.

PHIL

    Can I come in?

RACHEL

    Yeah.

Phil comes in and closes the door.

PHIL

    Alright? Is that any good? (*He means the book.*)

RACHEL

    Yeah – it's alright.

Pause.

PHIL

    Got any spare change?

RACHEL

    Yeah – I might 'ave a bit.

PHIL

    Only, it's me wossername – got to pay it tomorrow.

RACHEL

Yeah . . . 'course.

PHIL

Don't want to leave you short.

RACHEL

No – no, it's alright. (*She starts to get out of bed.*)

PHIL

It's alright – I'll get it.

RACHEL

Okay.

She stays in bed. Phil turns towards the door.

PHIL

Where's your purse?

RACHEL

It's downstairs.

PHIL

In yer coat?

RACHEL

Yeah.

She watches him go, then returns to her book.

A few moments later he pads up the stairs.

Now in Rachel's room, she empties her small change into her hand.

RACHEL

It's not much.

Phil holds out his hands. She puts the money into them.

PHIL

It all helps. Are you sure?

RACHEL

Yeah.

PHIL

What about your dinner money?

RACHEL

No, it's alright – I've still got a fiver.

PHIL

I'll give it back to you.

RACHEL

Okay.

PHIL

Thanks, love. Goodnight.

RACHEL

'Night.

Phil leaves the room, closing the door behind him. He pauses on the landing.

Penny is sitting up in bed, doing a crossword. She is wearing her spectacles. Phil comes in quietly, closes the door and moves round the bed.

PHIL

I should've just got 'alf a tank.

He shovels up some loose change by his side of the bed. Penny doesn't look at him.

'T's Friday tomorrow.

PENNY

Yeah, I know.

PHIL

I ain't 'ad a very good week this week.

PENNY

Ain't yer?

She half-looks at him.

PHIL

No . . .

He uncrumples a five-pound note and looks at it. Penny looks away.

Got any spare?

PENNY

Er, yeah – I, I got a bit, but . . . it ain't never spare, is it?

PHIL

Can I borrow some?

Penny says nothing. She still isn't looking at him.

I'll pay you back at the weekend.

Pause. Then she looks at him.

PENNY

Why don't you get up earlier in the mornings? Drive people to work, take 'em to the airport?

PHIL

Yeah, I know what you mean.

PENNY

'T's downstairs in me bag, in me bike-basket.

PHIL

Shall I take it out?

PENNY

No, bring it up.

PHIL

Alright.

He goes out. She watches him go. She puts down her pen. She is not happy.

A few moments later, Phil climbs the stairs again.

In the bedroom. He is sitting on the bed. Penny takes her purse out of her bag.

PHIL

I only need a tenner.

She takes it out and gives it to him.

Ta. 'Ave you got any change?

She looks in her purse.

PENNY

Yeah, I got a bit. Ain't much, though.

She tips it into his hands.

PHIL

That should do it.

Penny returns the purse to her bag. Then she puts the bag on the floor.

D'you want me to take that downstairs for you?

PENNY

No. (*She puts on her spectacles, and returns her attention to the crossword.*)

PHIL

Gi's a clue, then.

PENNY

Erm . . . 'Biblical son of Isaac; five letters, starting with a J.'

PHIL

Jonah.

PENNY

Oh, yeah. (*She starts to write.*)

PHIL

No, it ain't . . . 's wossername . . . Jacob.

PENNY

Are you sure?

PHIL

Yeah.

PENNY

'S thousand-pound prize.

PHIL

Is it?

PENNY

Yeah.

PHIL

No, I ain't sure, then.

Penny sighs.

Gi's another one.

PENNY

No, I'm gonna go asleep now. (*She takes off her spectacles and puts them in their case.*)

PHIL

Alright. (*He gets up.*) Be up in a minute. 'Night. (*He closes the door.*)

PENNY

'Night. (*She turns off her light and lies down with a sigh.*)

At the bottom of the stairs, Phil stops to count all his change.

Later, in bed, in the dark, Penny is awake. She is restless. Phil is snoring. Penny looks at him. Then she pushes back the duvet, and gets out of bed. Phil wakes up.

PHIL

Are you alright?

PENNY

Yeah.

PHIL

Are you goin' downstairs for a bit?

PENNY

Yeah.

Phil turns over and goes back to sleep.

On the balcony. Lit by the railway station below, Penny sits in an old chair. She is very sad. After a while, she looks back into the flat, in the direction of Phil and the bedroom. Then she sips a drink from a mug.

Next day. Bright sunlight. The care home, in the lounge. Rachel dusts an armchair, then a table. A middle-aged male cleaner in spectacles is using a vacuum cleaner. An elderly lady sits in a chair, gazing vacantly about. A small old man holding a newspaper walks slowly out of an adjacent dining room, where people are having breakfast.

RACHEL
(*to the small man*)

Mornin', 'Arold.

HAROLD
(*glumly*)

Mornin'.

Harold moves away. The male cleaner has turned off the vacuum cleaner, and now sits on a piano stool, mopping his face with his handkerchief. He is Sid. Rachel passes him.

RACHEL

Are you alright?

SID

Sweating like a pig, en' I?

A large lady Care Worker bustles past, and goes into the dining area.

CARE WORKER

Havin' a breather, Sid?

SID

Mm.

He gets up and goes over to Rachel, who is dusting a television set.

Ain't you 'ot, then?

RACHEL

No.

SID

Well, you're lucky.

More face-mopping.

Are you workin' at the weekend?

RACHEL

Yeah. (*She dusts another armchair.*)

SID

Just you and me then, innit?

Rachel moves to the piano. Sid follows her.

You make sure you go to bed early tonight then, eh?

Rachel dusts the piano. Sid moves away. The large care worker returns from the dining area, pushing an old man in a wheelchair.

CARE WORKER

Mind your elbow, honey.

Rachel carries on dusting.

Phil is in his bed, asleep, in broad daylight. He is snoring.

The crash-repair garage. Ron is standing by the near of his car, wearing his shades. He is counting some paper money. The Owner joins him.

RON

Looks good.

The Owner pats the car enthusiastically.

Hundred and fifty.

He gives the Owner the money.

OWNER
(*taking it*)

Hundred and eighty.

RON

You said one-fifty.

OWNER

Overnight service, Ron.

Peeved, Ron hands over the extra money. The Owner gives him his car keys.

Sorry. (*going*) Drive safe.

Ron moves towards the car.

Later. Ron has just parked the car outside the mini-cab office. He goes inside. Neville appears at an inner doorway.

NEVILLE
You was out of order yesterday – you know that?

Ron doesn't reply, but pulls out some more paper money and hands it to Neville, who takes it.

Well out of order.

He counts the money, gives Ron a dirty look, and disappears into his private office.

A few moments later. Phil crosses the road. He stops briefly to look at Ron's repair, then comes into the mini-cab office. Dinah is on the phone. Behind her, Neville is just sitting down at his desk.

DINAH
Yeah? . . . From over the chip shop?

PHIL
(*quietly*)

Mornin'.

Dinah gives him a half-smile.

DINAH
(*into phone*)
Deptford – yeah. I know.

Phil glances towards Ron, who is making himself a cup of tea. Phil wanders through to him.

PHIL
Alright, Ron?

RON

Yeah.

PHIL

He didn't let you down, then?

RON

No, 'e didn't. (*He removes his tea bag, and disposes of it.*)

PHIL

Good.

He goes over to Neville's desk. Neville is smoking a fag.

Alright, Nev? I've got your rent. That's –

Neville snatches some paper money from Phil's hand.

Sixty . . .

Neville counts it quickly.

NEVILLE

So where's the rest?

Phil hands him some coins.

PHIL

Eight pound coins.

Neville slams these on the desk.

NEVILLE

Bumba hole!

Phil dips into his trouser pocket.

PHIL

Twelve . . . in change. (*He holds out the small change.*)

NEVILLE

Where are you goin' with that?

The telephone rings.

PHIL

Yeah – sorry, Nev.

Dinah answers the phone. Her dialogue in this scene now overlaps with Neville's and Phil's.

NEVILLE

I done tell you already – I don't deal in shekels.

DINAH

Gladiator Cars, Dinah speakin' – how can I help?

NEVILLE

Go to the bank, man! Sick in my stomach!

DINAH

Yeah?

Phil pulls two one-pound coins out of the pile in his hand, and puts them on the desk.

PHIL

Take two now, and, er . . . I'll owe you a tenner.

DINAH

Pickin' up from . . . ? Tresillion . . . (*She writes it down.*) Yeah – five minutes.

NEVILLE

Look: if you're gonna rent my radios, show me some respect.

DINAH

Yeah, I can guarantee you five minutes.

PHIL

Yeah, I'll drop it off later.

NEVILLE

Give me proper money, man! Tchuh!

DINAH

I'll phone you when the driver's outside your house.

PHIL

Whatever. (*He heads for the door.*)

DINAH

Am I bein' abusive though?!

She slams down the receiver. Phil leaves.

NEVILLE

Wait . . . why you slam down the phone for? Why, you have
a bad attitude, sa. From I born!

Outside the care home (a name board: 'Brook House Resource Centre').

*Rachel and a care worker open the double doors, and out comes an
elderly lady, driving herself in an electric invalid buggy.*

OLD LADY

Thank you. 'Bye.

*She steers herself slowly round the corner of the building. Rachel, who
is wearing her street coat, overtakes her.*

RACHEL

See yer.

*The old lady smiles, and Rachel walks on, up the leafy street. It is still
a sunny day.*

*In a café. Samantha sits at an empty table, playing with her hair, and
chewing some gum. Donna finishes wiping a nearby table, then comes
over to Samantha.*

DONNA

'Scuse me.

*She leans across Samantha, and wipes her table. It is obvious that this
is where she works.*

SAMANTHA
(*sarcastic*)

Thank you!

DONNA
(*sarcastic*)

You're welcome.

She sits down opposite Samantha. Pause.

SAMANTHA

What?

DONNA

Nothing.

SAMANTHA

Got a problem?

DONNA

No, I ain't got a problem.

SAMANTHA

Ain't yer?

DONNA

Why should I 'ave a problem?

SAMANTHA

D'you 'ave a good time last night?

DONNA

Yeah, I did, actually.

SAMANTHA

Are you sure?

DONNA

Yeah, I am sure.

SAMANTHA

Are you?

DONNA

Yeah.

SAMANTHA

That's good.

DONNA

Yeah, it is good.

SAMANTHA

Where'd 'e take you, then?

DONNA

Never you mind.

SAMANTHA

Somewhere nice, was it?

DONNA

Yeah, it was, actually.

SAMANTHA

I reckon you got a bit of a problem.

DONNA

Like what?

SAMANTHA
(*indicating*)

You got a customer.

Donna looks.

DONNA

Fuck's sake!

She snatches up her cleaning cloth, and goes off to the counter, where Rachel has just arrived.

RACHEL
(*to Donna*)

Alright?

DONNA

Alright? (*She goes behind the counter.*)

RACHEL

Just a Coke, please.

A few moments later, Rachel comes over to Samantha's corner.

Alright?

Samantha doesn't reply. Rachel sits at an adjacent empty table. She pours her Coke into a tumbler. Samantha has a can of Diet Coke and no tumbler. Pause.

SAMANTHA

Just come from work, then, 'ave yer?

RACHEL

Yeah. (*Pause.*) What've you been up to, then?

SAMANTHA

Not a lot – just got up. (*Pause.*) What d'you 'ave to do, then? At work?

RACHEL

Cleanin'.

Donna returns to Samantha's table.

SAMANTHA

What, you 'ave to . . . wipe down the old grandads, 'n' that?

RACHEL

No, it's not my job.

SAMANTHA

'Oo does that, then?

RACHEL

Carers.

Donna is lighting a fag.

DONNA

It's disgustin'. I'm glad it's not my job.

SAMANTHA

'T's better than workin' 'ere, though, innit?

DONNA

Yeah, but at least I've got a job!

SAMANTHA
(under her breath)

Fuck off!

DONNA

What about when they die?

Samantha grimaces – in disapproval of the question.

RACHEL

Well . . . just gotta clear out their room.

Samantha and Donna each reflect on this. Then Samantha's eye goes to the window. Craig is just arriving outside. He looks at her. She blanks him, and he moves away.

Early evening. In Phil's car, in a traffic jam. A youngish, slightly neurotic woman with dyed red hair and in a very low-cut strapless dress is in the back seat. London accent.

NEUROTIC WOMAN

How much d'you think it's gonna be?

PHIL

About fourteen, fifteen . . .

NEUROTIC WOMAN

Okay.

PHIL

Is that alright?

NEUROTIC WOMAN

Yeah. What? You think I ain't got it?

PHIL
(innocently)

Eh?

She is obviously deeply offended by something Phil hasn't said. She seethes with indignation for a while, shaking her head in disbelief.

Night in Phil's car. His passenger is in the front seat. A grubby fellow in his mid-forties. Clutching a whisky bottle. Very drunk. Manchester accent.

DRUNK

Oh . . . fuck it. I mean, what – it's er, all the stuff that . . .
I mean, it all – y'know, like – it was supposed to . . . an'
'e was gonna bring round the . . . just fuckin', just kept
thinkin' . . . too much, y'know. (*He sighs.*) I mean, I don't
know 'ow it, y'know – you seem like a nice bloke. An'
erm . . . Oh, fuckin' wanker, y'know? Fuckin' . . . what
can you . . . ? Are we, um . . . ? (*He points.*) Round there,
they used to, er . . . someone . . . see that door there?
It used to open, inwards.

PHIL

Yeah?

DRUNK

I should 'ave, er . . . should 'ave done somethin' else.

Meanwhile, Penny is on her balcony with a mug of tea. That worried look again. Railway sounds from nearby.

Next day. The care home. In the staff room. Bright sunlight. Rachel is making a cup of tea. Sid is sitting next to her, smoking a fag.

SID

Did you go to bed early, then?

RACHEL

About tennish.

SID

Tennish. That is early.

The large Care Worker rushes into the room and takes a diet crispbread out of a packet on a shelf.

CARE WORKER

I'm starvin'.

RACHEL

Kettle's just boiled.

CARE WORKER

Ain't on a break.

She rushes out, taking a bite of crispbread as she goes. Rachel moves across the room with her tea.

SID

I can't remember the last time I was in bed by ten. About 1950, I should think.

Rachel sits on a sofa and sips her tea.

One o'clock, me . . . if I'm lucky. Two. 'Alf three, sometimes. Then 'alf an hour later, I'm pacin' about. Then I make meself a cuppa tea. Drop off in the chair. (*He breaks some wrapped chocolate in half, and puts one bit on the coffee table.*) 'Ere. I'd give a year's wages for a good night's sleep.

He eats his chocolate. Rachel takes hers. It's green Aero.

RACHEL

Thanks.

SID

I bet you'll be up late tonight, though, won't you, with your boyfriend? Saturday night?

RACHEL

I ain't got a boyfriend. You know that.

SID

What d'you drink, then? Lager?

RACHEL

Yeah.

SID

Coupla pints'll do me. Fish an' chips. Saturday night.

That night. In Rachel's living room. She sits alone, in the middle of the sofa, reading her book. Silence.

In Donna's bedroom. She is sitting on the bed, wearing a vest and a very short skirt. Jason is standing over her, moving his knee around between her legs. He is wearing a shirt and jeans, and is smoking a fag.

> DONNA
>
> What're you doin'?

> JASON
>
> What does it look like I'm doin'?

> DONNA
>
> I dunno . . . That's why I'm askin' yer.

> JASON
>
> Oh, what – ain't I allowed to touch you no more?

> DONNA
>
> I ain't sayin' that.

> JASON
>
> Eh?

He smacks her face, lightly but aggressively.

> DONNA
>
> Ge' off!! (*Pause.*) Gi's some o'that (*his fag*).

> JASON
>
> Well, you – you got your own there. (*He indicates the cupboard.*)

> DONNA
>
> I don't want one o' me own. Come on!

> JASON
>
> No.

He holds his fag behind his back for a moment – a kind of game. Then he lets her have it.

> Fuck's sake.

He goes to smack her again, but she deflects him with a slap.

DONNA

Don't punch me!

Jason hits her in the face – as before, lightly but aggressively.

JASON

Don't 'it *me*! Right, an' another thing, right? Don't you dare phone me at 'alf eleven at night, right?

DONNA

I texted yer. You never phoned me back.

JASON

Oh, fuck that – No, I'm out with the boys, right, you're showin' me up, you're makin' a right mug o'me.

DONNA

That's your problem, innit?

JASON

I was gonna get back to yer, wa'n' I?

DONNA

Was yer?

JASON

O' course I fuckin' was – just relax.

DONNA

You relax.

JASON

Oh, fuck . . . (*He sits next to her on the bed.*) Right, so what we doin', then? – we goin' out, or what?

DONNA

Stayin' in.

JASON

Oh, we're stayin' in, yeah? That's nice, innit, eh? Eh?

He strokes her hair – which action quickly becomes pushing her head around aggressively.

DONNA

Ge' *off*!!

JASON

Come 'ere. (*He lies back on the bed.*)

DONNA

No.

JASON

Fuckin' come 'ere!

DONNA

No, I don't wanna.

He laughs ironically.

JASON

You love it, don't you, eh?

DONNA

Wha'?

JASON

I swear to God, right, you are the biggest cock-teaser I've ever met in my life.

DONNA

Fuck off – I ain't no cock-teaser!

JASON

'Ow d'you get that bruise?

DONNA

You done it.

JASON

Good.

He sits up and prods his finger into the bruise, which is on Donna's thigh, and is quite big.

Does it 'urt, does it, eh?

DONNA

No.

JASON

Fuckin' 'urts?

DONNA

No.

A sexual, more good-humoured spark. Donna kicks off her shoes.
Jason lies back. Donna leans across him to stub out the fag.

A little later. They are having lively sex under the duvet. Donna sits up
suddenly.

JASON

What're you doin'?

DONNA

Nothin'.

JASON

What's the matter?

DONNA

I'm alright.

JASON

What, you don't like the way I'm doin' it to yer?

DONNA

Yeah.

Pause.

JASON

Stop playin' about, Donna.

DONNA

I ain't playin' about.

JASON

Well, just lay down.

He tries to push her down.

DONNA

I don't wanna lay down!!

JASON

Just lay the fuck down!!

He forces her down, but she sits up.

DONNA

I don't wanna fuckin' lay down with yer!!

Pause.

JASON

Oh, what? You – you don't wanna do it no more?

DONNA

I ain't sayin' that.

JASON

Eh?

DONNA

I ain't sayin' that.

JASON

No, no, no, just tell me – you don't wanna do it no more.

Pause. Donna doesn't reply.

Oh, fuck this. (*He jumps out of bed.*)

DONNA

Where are you goin'?

JASON

No, no, I'm gettin' out of 'ere, right?

During the following, he gets dressed.

I don't need this. (*A sarcastic chuckle.*) D'you know what
I mean? I make the effort. I drive all the way round 'ere –
nearly two miles . . . Like, we're gettin' it on on the bed an'
all that, right? – sweet, lovely . . . and you go all cold on me.
I mean, you blow all 'ot an' cold, Donna, like some fuckin'
tap.

Donna shakes her head.

D'you know 'ow that makes me feel? Eh? Oh, t'rific, lovely.
Thanks very much. I can go somewhere else. Donna –

right? I'll go down the pub, with the boys. Yeah? Right?
I don't give a fuck. Fuckin' *end of*! Fuckin' little bitch.

DONNA

I don't want you to go.

JASON

Yeah, well, I'm goin', en' I?

DONNA

I wanna talk to yer.

JASON

What d'you wanna talk about? I don't wanna talk, I wanna
shag.

DONNA

Well, I do wanna talk – I wanna tell you somethin'.

JASON

Well, what d'you wanna tell me, for fuck's sake?

DONNA

I'm pregnant.

JASON

What? Say that again.

DONNA

I'm pregnant.

Pause.

JASON

No, you ain't pregnant – you're on the pill.

DONNA

I know I'm on the pill, but I'm 'avin' a baby.

JASON

Bollocks.

DONNA

'T's yours.

JASON

You – no, you're 'avin' a fuckin' laugh.

DONNA

It's not very funny, is it?

JASON

No, 'ow d'you know?

DONNA

What? 'Ow do I know I'm pregnant?

JASON

Yeah – 'ow d'you know you're pregnant?

DONNA

I went up the doctor's.

JASON

When?

DONNA

Two weeks ago.

JASON

Two weeks –?

DONNA

Yeah.

JASON
(*shouting*)

You've fuckin' known for two weeks an' you didn't bother to tell me?!

DONNA
(*shouting*)

I 'aven't seen you for two weeks, 'ave I?

JASON
(*shouting*)

Bollocks . . . ! You seen me on Thursday!!

DONNA
(*shouting*)

When I do, you're always shoutin' at me!

JASON
(*frightened*)

Fuckin' 'ell, Donna!!

Donna looks helpless.

Oh, for fuck's sake.

A pub. Karaoke night. The place is full. Penny, Maureen and Carol are sitting round a table. Penny and Maureen have pints of lager, Carol a large vodka and tonic. The MC, an overweight middle-aged guy, is singing 'Delilah' by Les Reed and Barry Mason. This carries on throughout the scene. Here are the words . . .

My, my, my, Delilah!
Why, why, why, Delilah?
I could see
That girl was no good for me.
But I was lost like a slave that no man could free.

At break of day,
When that man drove away,

I was waiting.
I crossed the street to her house
And she opened the door.
She stood there laughing.
I felt the knife in my hand and she laughed no more.

My, my, my, Delilah!
Why, why, why, Delilah?
So, before
They come to break down the door,
Forgive me, Delilah –
I just couldn't take any more!

Maureen joins in the second line of the song –

MAUREEN
– why, Delilah? (*cupping her hand*)
Duh duh-duh-duh-duh-duh!

Penny watches Carol taking a long swig of her drink. Her head slumps forward.

Alright, Carol?

Maureen has a swig of beer. Carol looks up.

CAROL
What's that look for?

MAUREEN
What look?

CAROL
You gi's a fuckin' look.

MAUREEN
No, I ain't.

CAROL
Yeah, you did.

MAUREEN
(*slight laugh*)
You gettin' the 'ump again?

CAROL

I ain't got the 'ump.

MAUREEN

Don't get stroppy with me.

CAROL

I ain't gettin' stroppy with yer.

MAUREEN

Ain't yer?

CAROL

No.

MAUREEN

I'm yer mate. We're all mates, ain't we?

PENNY

Yeah.

MAUREEN
(to Carol)

There y'are – see?

65

*Carol immediately becomes tearful and remorseful. She strokes
Maureen's shoulder.*

CAROL

Don't take no fuckin' notice of me.

MAUREEN
(*warmly*)

I ain't takin' no notice of yer.

CAROL

You been a good friend to me, Maureen.

MAUREEN

Yeah, I 'ave.

CAROL

I love you.

*She takes Maureen's face in her hands. Maureen puts her hands
around Carol's – more by way of trying to break loose than reciprocally.*

MAUREEN

I love you too, Carol.

CAROL
(*emotionally*)

Do you?

MAUREEN

Yeah.

She signals subtly ('Rescue me') to Penny.

PENNY

Yeah, 't's alright, Carol!

She touches Carol's shoulder.

CAROL

Penny!!

She swings round to Carol, touching her chin.

Pretty girl . . .

MAUREEN

Your turn!

D'you love me?

Pause.

PENNY
(*unconvincingly*)

Yeah . . .

Maureen laughs.

Donna and Maureen's flat. Donna is coming down the stairs. Her duvet is wrapped around her. Jason stands at the bottom of the stairs.

JASON

I bet you stopped takin' the pill on purpose, didn't yer?

DONNA

Of course I never!

JASON

That's exactly what you'd do, Donna – just to fuckin' keep me.

DONNA

Oh, you think so, do yer?

JASON

Swear on yer mum's grave!

DONNA

She ain't dead yet!

JASON

Right, I mean it, right – if I ever found out you did that to me, I'D FUCKING KILL YOU, YOU SLAG!!!

DONNA

GO ON THEN – KILL ME!!

Pause. Jason is briefly lost for words. Donna sits on the stairs.

JASON

. . . Fuck! . . . Listen to me, right? This doesn't 'ave to be a big thing.

DONNA

It *is* a big thing!

JASON

No, it ain't, Donna . . . This 'appens all the time to people.
All you gotta do . . . is you go, and you get rid of it. Yeah?
I ain't gonna be a wanker. I'll give you a little bit of money
and, y'know, I'll come along to the place and sort it with you.

DONNA

That's nice of you, innit?

JASON

It's done and dusted then, Donna.

DONNA

Just like that.

JASON

Yeah – simple.

DONNA

Simple!

JASON

I mean it, right? If you keep it, I'm fuckin' walkin'. If you
wanna stay with me, you fuckin' get rid of it, right?

DONNA

And that's it, is it?

JASON

What d'you wanna 'ave a kid for, Donna, right? (*violently,
smacking one hand with the other*) 'Ow're yer gonna feed it?
'Ow're yer gonna support it? I don't wanna be a dad,
Donna, right? I don't wanna do it! I ain't up to it! I don't
even wanna be with you!!

DONNA

Fuck off!!

JASON

(*backing down the stairs*)

Yeah . . . Yeah, I've been, I've been thinkin' about it for
a coupla months now, thinkin' about jackin' it all in, to be
honest with yer. 'Cos all we ever do when we get together,

Donna, is fuckin' argue, innit? In't that the truth? It's doin' my fuckin' 'ead in!!

Pause. Donna is fraught and shocked. Jason comes back up the stairs at her.

You know when I went up to Newcastle . . . with Cooky and the boys? Yeah, we was in a club . . . I pulled the best little bit of pussy ever. In the toilets, yeah –

DONNA
(*smacking his face*)

Fuck off!!

JASON
(*shouting*)

Don't you dare!!

Pause.

She 'ad a lovely pair of tits, tight arse; an' I tell you what: she gave me the best fuckin' blow-job I've ever 'ad in my life. Ten times better than you could ever give it!

Pause.

Oh, what, what, what – are you gonna start cryin' now, are yer?

DONNA
(*crying*)

I'm not cryin'.

JASON

No, go on, cry – go on, let it all out!

DONNA

Fuck off!

JASON

I mean it, Donna – you lumber me with a kid, you won't know what's 'it yer!! (*shouting*) I'll make your life shit!!

DONNA
(*shouting*)

You already do!!

Jason opens the door violently and slams it against the wall.

JASON

I'll bury you, you cunt!! Fuckin' mug!!

He storms off into the night, leaving the door wide open. Donna sits tearful and helpless on her stairs.

Back at the Karaoke, Maureen is arriving at the table with a round of drinks. The singer is a youngish blonde woman. The song is 'Stand By Your Man' by Tammy Wynette and Billy Sherrill. It has already begun. Here are the words we hear . . .

But if you love him,
You'll forgive him,
Even though he's hard to understand.
And if you love him,
Be proud of him,
'Cos, after all, he's just a man.

Stand by your man.
Give him two arms to cling to.
And something warm to come to
When nights are cold and lonely.
Stand by your man.

And show the world you love him –
Keep giving all the love you can.
Stand by your man.

Maureen has sat down. They all take their drinks.

MAUREEN

Cheers, girls.

PENNY

Cheers.

CAROL

Take this off! (*She is referring to Maureen's cardigan.*)

MAUREEN

In a minute.

CAROL

'As it got sleeves?

MAUREEN

No, it's sleeveless.

CAROL

Take it off!

Maureen reluctantly takes it off.

Oh, it's nice, innit? D'yer get it out of the catalogue?

MAUREEN

I got the cardigan out o' the catalogue – I got the top in the market. They don't match – they're odd.

CAROL
(*rubbing Maureen's bottom*)
Sexy girl. (*to Penny*) Don't she look sexy?

PENNY

Yeah.

MAUREEN

You gonna 'ave a sing?

CAROL

I'll get up in a bit. I'm gonna 'ave a laugh later.

PENNY

You got a good voice, then?

CAROL

Fuckin' sight better than 'er. Dolly Parton, me.

She pulls down her top to expose more cleavage.

SINGER

Give him two arms to cling to,
And something warm to come to
When nights are cold and lonely . . .

MAUREEN

You gonna 'ave a sing?

PENNY

No, it's too embarrassing.

CAROL

'Ow long you been married, Penny?

PENNY

I ain't married.

CAROL

Ain't yer?

MAUREEN

No, she ain't.

CAROL

Why ain't yer?

PENNY

I dunno. Never asked me.

MAUREEN

Don't matter, does it?

PENNY

No, I ain't bothered.

CAROL

What a cunt.

MAUREEN

Oh, that's nice!

PENNY

I wouldn't want to get married in a church, anyway.

CAROL

Oh, I got married in a church. It was lovely. It was the best day of my fuckin' life. My little Ronnie . . . sweet'eart.

The song ends. Everybody claps and cheers. Except Carol, who is lost in her memories as she downs her vodka.

In Phil's car. Late. Two Party Girls in skimpy dresses are in the back seat. One is adjusting something about her person. The other one speaks.

FIRST PARTY GIRL

Oh, fuckin' 'ell!! Don't touch it, because it'll make it worse.

SECOND PARTY GIRL

What's it –?

FIRST PARTY GIRL

No, leave it, 'cos it's right on your nipple.

The Second Party Girl breaks into a peal of giggles.

SECOND PARTY GIRL

My fuckin' nipple . . .!

FIRST PARTY GIRL

No, leave it – I'm not kidd– I'm not touchin' your nipple.

Phil keeps on driving.

Back at the Karaoke. The MC is holding the microphone.

MC

Ladies and gentlemen, give a big, warm welcome to our next singer: put your hands together for – Maureen! Come on down, Maureen!

MAUREEN

Oh, blimey! My turn!

She gets up amidst applause, and goes to the stage. As Penny claps she looks over and sees Carol, who is staggering around by the bar, carrying a vodka in each hand. She is now very drunk. As she takes a swig from one tumbler, Penny comes over and relieves her of the other, then tries to get her to sit down to listen to Maureen. Carol resists. Penny sits down. As the intro plays, Maureen gives a victory salute to Carol, who waves back, and goes into a solo reverie – a sort of sexy dance.

Maureen sings cheerfully and confidently and with real musical ability. She only occasionally needs to glance at the words of the lyric, which is 'Don't It Make My Brown Eyes Blue?' by Richard Leigh.

MAUREEN
(*sings*)
Don't know when I've been so blue . . .
Don't know what's come over you . . .

She smiles at Penny, who returns a tiny smile.

You've found someone new,
And don't it make my brown eyes blue?
I'll be fine when you are gone –
I'll just cry the whole night long . . .
Say it isn't true,
And don't it make my brown eyes blue?
Tell me no secrets, tell me no lies;
Give me no reasons, give me alibis . . .

Penny watches anxiously as Carol now starts groping a guy sitting on a bar stool. She tries to get him to dance. He is not responsive. Carol collapses on the floor, dragging him down with her, to the sound of breaking glass. During this, Maureen has carried on singing . . . .

Tell me you love me, and don't say goodbye.*
Say anything, but don't say goodbye –

This is the point at which Carol collapses. Maureen immediately stops singing, hands the microphone to the MC, and goes to Carol's rescue. So does Penny.

PENNY
Carol!

General chaos. Carol is suffering and inert. A big guy struggles unsuccessfully to help her to her feet. Several other people try to be useful.

MAUREEN
Mind 'er arms, mind 'er arms!

The MC makes an announcement about everybody keeping calm. Another young woman tries to help.

PENNY
Come and sit down.

* This line should be 'and don't make me cry'. Maureen gets it wrong.

MAUREEN

It's alright – I've got you!

Maureen and Penny carry Carol across the room. She is gasping and helpless.

PENNY

Come on, you've got to walk – Carol!

In Phil's car at the dead of night on a main road. Three thirty-something trendy types are stoned out of their heads, two women in the back, a guy in the front. One of the women, a blonde, weeps quietly. The other dozes a bit. The guy has shades perched on the top of his head and a supercilious smirk on his face. He takes a deep drag on his fag. Phil coughs. The blonde blows her nose. Nobody speaks. Phil keeps on driving.

Meanwhile, somewhere on the estate, Samantha walks across a stretch of grass. Craig watches her through a fence. As she approaches, he scuttles off. He stands by a wall.

SAMANTHA
(*arriving*)

What're you doin'? Waitin' for someone, are yer?

She joins him.

What's that?

CRAIG

What?

SAMANTHA

That.

She prods a finger at his face.

CRAIG

I cut myself.

SAMANTHA

Did yer?

CRAIG

Shavin' . . .

SAMANTHA

Oh, you've 'ad a shave, 'ave yer?

CRAIG

Yeah – razor.

SAMANTHA

Tryin' a look nice for someone, are yer?

CRAIG
(*defensive*)

Nah.

SAMANTHA

Why, don't you fancy no one?

Craig chortles.

What's that?

No reply.

What?

82

She moves away to the end of the wall, and leans on it with her back to him. He follows her. When he reaches her, she moves away again. It becomes clear that the wall is the side of the first of a row of dilapidated lock-up garages. She leans against a metal door. The graffiti says 'NOW'. Craig approaches her slowly.

SAMANTHA

What're you lookin' at?

She is, as usual, wearing a revealing low neckline and a collection of necklaces. Craig is looking at these.

CRAIG

Is that real gold?

SAMANTHA

Yeah.

She moves close to him. He breathes heavily.

What?

He lurches forward to kiss her, but she moves away.

What's that, a kiss?

CRAIG

No.

SAMANTHA
(*smirking*)

What was it, then?

She moves away a little distance, then stops. He follows her, and again he tries to kiss her. And again she moves away.

You got bad breath, ain't yer?

She walks some distance, past several garages. A dog barks nearby. She stops.

Ain't yer never kissed no one before? Eh?

Craig stops a few feet away from her, and puts a fresh fag in his mouth. Suddenly, Samantha lurches at him, takes the fag out of his mouth, and kisses him on the lips. He responds. She tries to back off, but he keeps the kiss going. She breaks loose.

Alright!

He grabs hold of her hair, and she pushes him off violently. He staggers back.

Ow! Don't fuckin' touch!!

She moves back to him.

I can touch you . . . but you can't touch me. Alright?

She pulls his hair. Then she strokes it for a few moments.

Like that, do you? Yeah?

Now he lurches forward again, and pins her against an old car – the last garage is open. They struggle briefly, then she throws him off.

Fuck off!!

CRAIG

You don't know!

SAMANTHA

What?! What don't I know? You're sick! You're a fuckin' pervert!

She stomps off into the night. Craig remains standing by the car, helpless.

Somewhere else on the estate. Rory sits alone in the dark on a low wall, smoking a fag.

And Phil is in his car. It is stationary.

PHIL

That's six pounds, please.

He rubs his eyes – he's tired. Pause.

Then a bearded guy in his mid-thirties sits up in the back seat and puts his face in his hands.

PASSENGER

Fuck! Oh . . .

PHIL

You alright?

The guy uncovers his face. He keeps sniffing.

PASSENGER

I ain't got any money.

PHIL

What, you ain't got nothin'?

PASSENGER

Look. I'm really, really, really, truly sorry, but . . . I ain't got a bean.

Pause. Phil rubs his eyes.

PHIL

Go on, then. Go on, piss off.

The Fare Dodger gets out of the car immediately.

Life's too short.

Phil drives off. He speaks into his walkie-talkie.

One-three . . .

Phil and Penny's living room. On the floor are the remains of a late-night snack – a plate, a tumbler, an empty crisp bag, etc. Phil stops by these, then goes to the sofa, where Penny is asleep, fully clothed. He touches her gently. She wakes up with a start.

PENNY

Cor!! (*She looks at Phil.*) What're you doin'?

PHIL

You was asleep.

PENNY

Yeah, I know I was asleep.

PHIL

'S three o'clock in the mornin'.

PENNY

It ain't, is it?

PHIL

It's five past.

Penny rests her head on the arm of the sofa.

PENNY

Oh – ow!

PHIL

Are you stiff?

PENNY
(*sitting up*)

Yeah – ooh! (*She holds her head.*)

PHIL

D'you 'ave a good time?

PENNY

No, if you must know. (*She sees the stuff on the floor.*) Oh, Rory's back, then. I was waitin' up for 'im.

PHIL

I got your money. You gave me a tenner . . . (*He puts a banknote beside her.*) I didn't 'ave a bad night, as it 'appens.

PENNY

Makes a change.

PHIL

And the rest came to – (*counting out coins*) – four pound twenty – no, twenty-one . . . no, no – twenty-six.

PENNY

Not now, Phil.

PHIL

Right. I'll put it on the sideboard. (*He collects up the money.*)

Next morning in the care home. Rachel knocks on a door bearing the name-tag 'Martha George'. She opens the door. An elderly lady with white hair is lying in bed. The sun streams in through the curtains.

RACHEL

Mornin'!

MARTHA
(*stirring*)

Mmm??

RACHEL

You alright?

MARTHA
(*half-sitting up*)

Mm? Oh . . . oh. What's the time?

RACHEL

It's just gone 'alf eight.

Martha squints at her watch, which is on the bedside cupboard.

MARTHA

Oh . . .

RACHEL

You're a bit late this mornin'.

MARTHA

Oh . . . Sorry, Rachel.

RACHEL

No, it's alright – I'll go and do Bill first.

MARTHA

Just give me a minute.

RACHEL

Okay . . .

She closes the door and moves to the next room, the door of which is open. Sid ambles by. He stands by the door, watching Rachel. She makes the bed.

SID

I couldn't wear me pyjamas last night. Lay there, stark naked. Morning, Martha.

Martha is just going into an adjacent toilet.

MARTHA

Oh, 'ello. (*She closes the toilet door.*)

SID
(*to Rachel*)

What about you, eh?

Rachel looks at him.

RACHEL

It weren't that 'ot.

SID

Well, I was.

He moves away. Rachel continues to make the bed.

Maureen is coming up some outdoor steps on the estate. She is carrying a bunch of flowers. She comes across Donna sitting at the top of the steps.

MAUREEN

What're you sittin' there for?

DONNA

Forgot me key.

MAUREEN

You been cryin'? What's the matter? What's that on yer face? Someone 'it yer?

She holds back Donna's hair for a moment, revealing a black eye. Donna gets up and walks away. Maureen follows.

Donna!

She follows Donna along the walkway.

In Donna's bedroom. Donna is sitting on the bed. Maureen comes in and sits near her, also on the bed.

MAUREEN

I've put the kettle on. Now . . . What's goin' on? Eh? 'As 'e 'it yer? 'E 'as, an' 'e? Donna –?

DONNA

We 'ad a fight.

MAUREEN

What, a real fight or a pretend fight?

DONNA

It ain't funny.

MAUREEN

I ain't jokin' – 'e's a big bloke. You're only a little skinny thing.

DONNA

I ain't skinny!

MAUREEN

'Oo does 'e think 'e is, the bleedin' bully? What'd 'e 'it you for, anyway?

DONNA

I pushed 'im.

MAUREEN

You pushed im, so 'e 'it yer.

DONNA

Yeah.

MAUREEN

Nice. Better not show 'is face round 'ere again.

DONNA

Ain't none of your business.

MAUREEN

It is my business.

DONNA

It ain't!

MAUREEN

I knew 'e was no good.

DONNA

You never give 'im a chance.

MAUREEN

Never give 'im a chance? You never gave yourself a chance.
You've only known 'im a couple of months.

DONNA

Yeah, an' 'ow long did you know my dad, then?

MAUREEN

I dunno . . . about five minutes.

DONNA

Yeah, so shut up!

*Pause. Maureen reflects for a few moments. Donna watches her, then
looks away.*

MAUREEN

D'you love 'im?

Donna doesn't reply.

I don't want you to see 'im no more, 'e's trouble.

DONNA

Ain't as easy as that.

MAUREEN

What's that supposed to mean?

DONNA

Nothin'.

Pause. Maureen watches Donna thoughtfully.

Anyway, leave me alone. I can deal with it meself.

MAUREEN

You ain't pregnant, are yer?

Donna doesn't reply.

Oh, Donna. I thought you was on the pill.

DONNA

I am on the pill.

MAUREEN

Well, don't you take it no more?

85

DONNA

Yeah.

MAUREEN

'Ow far gone are yer?

DONNA

Two months.

MAUREEN

Two months . . . you tell 'im you're pregnant, so 'e 'its yer.

DONNA

It weren't like that.

MAUREEN

No? Well, what was it like, then?

DONNA

I dunno.

MAUREEN

I thought you 'ad more sense, Donna.

DONNA

Fuck off!!

MAUREEN

Oh, don't get the 'ump, you silly cow! Does yer face 'urt?

She holds back Donna's hair to have another look. Donna resists.

DONNA

Yeah.

MAUREEN

I'll make you a cuppa tea. (*She gets up.*) Want two sugars?

DONNA

Yeah.

Maureen goes downstairs. Donna gets her mobile out of her bag and proceeds to text a message.

Penny, Phil, Rachel and Rory are sitting around their table, eating their Sunday lunch. Phil sips some beer from a glass.

PENNY
(*to Rachel*)
'Ow was work today?

RACHEL
Alright.

Rory has finished his food. He puts his knife and fork on the plate.

RORY
That was shit. (*He gets up and lies on the sofa.*)

PENNY
Rory!

RORY
What?!

PENNY
There's no need to talk like that.

RORY
Fuck off!!

PENNY
Rory, will you stop bein' rude to me, please?

RORY
For fuck's sake!! What is your problem?!! (*He gets up.*) I only said I didn't like my dinner! I can't do nothin' round 'ere without you 'avin a go at me! You're doin' my fuckin' 'ead in – Why don't you fuck off?! (*He storms out of the room.*)

Pause.

PHIL
Take no notice.

Penny is shaken.

Inside a front door. Somebody knocks on it, hard and violent.
Maureen and Donna arrive together at it, Maureen from downstairs,
Donna from upstairs. Maureen opens it slightly. We hear, but initially
can't see, Jason.

MAUREEN

What d'you want?

JASON

Is Donna there, please?

MAUREEN

No, she ain't!

She closes the door on him, but he pushes it open.

JASON
(*simultaneously*)
Look, I know she's fuckin' there!!!

DONNA
(*simultaneously*)
Alright, Mum – I'll sort it!!!

MAUREEN
(*to Donna*)
Alright!

JASON
(*to Donna*)
Alright, so what's goin' on?

MAUREEN

If you ever touch my daughter again, I'll phone the police.

JASON

Fuck off!

MAUREEN

'Oo're you talking to?

JASON
(*shouting*)
Yeah, well, I ain't talkin' to you?

DONNA
(*shouting*)

Leave it, Mum!!

MAUREEN

No, I bleedin' won't!!

JASON

Right, just keep out of it, right, 'cos it's got fuck-all to do
with you!

MAUREEN

Ain't it? Look what you've done to 'er face!

JASON

Well, she's fuckin' askin' for it, ain't she?

MAUREEN

You coward!

JASON

Fuck off! She's coming round to my 'ouse, right,
threatening to tell me mum somethin'.

MAUREEN

Tell your mum what? That she's pregnant?

JASON

What?! (*He is thrown.*) What d'you tell 'er for, eh?

DONNA

'Cos she's me mum!

MAUREEN

That's it – get out of my 'ouse!!

She pushes him. He resists.

JASON

Get your fuckin' 'ands off me!

DONNA

Don't touch 'er!

JASON

Fucking . . .! I don't even wanna be here!

MAUREEN

What're yer doin' 'ere, then?

JASON

She texted me, right? Told me, 'Come over 'ere' – so 'ere
I am.

MAUREEN

D'you text 'im?

DONNA

Yeah.

JASON

So what's this big thing you gotta tell me, eh? What's the
great secret?

Pause. Maureen and Jason look at Donna. She turns away.

MAUREEN

She ain't got nothin' to say to you!!

She starts to close the door. He pushes it open.

JASON

Typical Donna, innit, eh? I tell you what, you're twisted in
the 'ead – you're fuckin' mental!!

Maureen closes the door on him.

MAUREEN

You leave 'er alone!

JASON
(*still resisting the door*)
An' I'll tell you what: she's the worst fuckin' shag I've 'ad in
my life!

MAUREEN

Yeah? She said the same about you. (*She slams the door shut.*)

JASON
(*from outside, shouting*)
I 'ad 'er in your bed an' all, you cunt!!

He kicks the door.

Fuckin' mug!!

Pause. He has gone.

MAUREEN
Bloody 'ell, Donna! You don't 'alf pick 'em!

She goes, leaving Donna standing there in pain.

Jason marches furiously across the estate in his shorts. He passes Samantha, who is sitting on a wall.

SAMANTHA
She dumped you then, 'as she?

JASON
(*not stopping*)
Oh, fuck off!

SAMANTHA
Where are you goin'?

JASON
I'm fuckin' getting out of 'ere, ain't I?

SAMANTHA
(*jumping up*)
Can I come?

He disappears behind a building. She follows him.

What's the matter? Don't you like me?!

Maureen and Donna's living room. Donna sits on the sofa. Maureen is in an armchair, flicking through a magazine. She is wearing her spectacles.

MAUREEN
'Ow're you feelin'?

DONNA
I'm alright.

MAUREEN

You're better off without 'im, you know.

DONNA

I know.

Maureen turns a page.

MAUREEN

You gonna keep the baby?

Pause.

DONNA

I dunno . . .

MAUREEN

What, you wanna 'ave an abortion?

DONNA

No.

Pause.

MAUREEN

You want somethin' to eat?

Donna doesn't reply.

You're eatin' for two now, you know.

DONNA

Shu' up!!

MAUREEN

I'll make yer two chips.

DONNA

Ha-ha!

MAUREEN

Suit yourself!

Pause.

When's your first 'ospital appointment?

I dunno.

MAUREEN
D'you want me to come with you?

DONNA
(*quietly*)
If you want.

MAUREEN
No fun goin' on your own. I know.

Night, in Jason's car, in the middle of nowhere – a field? Samantha is sitting astride Jason. She is naked from the waist up. She is taking off Jason's shirt.

SAMANTHA
Let's get this off.

JASON
Alright – Easy! Easy!

SAMANTHA
What about Donna?

JASON
What're you fuckin' thinkin' about 'er for?

SAMANTHA
I'm not thinkin' about 'er – Come on . . .

JASON
No – er, oi – what d'you say it for, then?

SAMANTHA
Well, she's gonna be pissed off, ain't she?

JASON
Look, right? I'm fuckin' telling you, right – don't –

Samantha giggles.

No, oi – don't mention 'er name again, yeah?

She is still trying to get off his top.

SAMANTHA

Why not?

JASON

Oh, fuckin' bollocks, right? I'm serious – get out the fuckin' car, yeah? I'll fuckin' drive 'ome an' leave you 'ere, yeah? Is that what you fuckin' want?

She giggles, and pushes his top over his head.

Fuckin' 'ell –

She kisses him on the lips, then works her way down to his chest.

You're a fuckin' nightmare, in't yer?

SAMANTHA

Yeah.

They go into a passionate session.

Next day. The care home, in a bathroom. Rachel is cleaning a blue walk-in bath for elderly people – the solid kind with a gate. Sid comes in.

SID

Alright?

Rachel doesn't reply. Sid goes and stands beside her. She carries on working.

I was married once, y'know.

RACHEL

Was yer?

SID

Yeah. Four months. Bitch. And she was a nurse. (*He sits on a chair.*) You get used to it.

Rachel opens the gate, and crouches down to clean the inside of the bath.

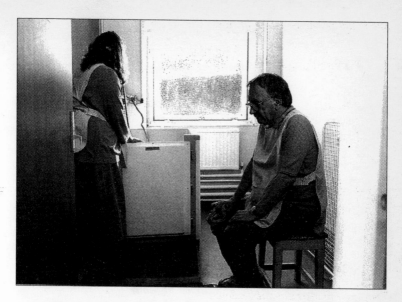

What're you doin' after work? D'you wanna go for a stroll in the park? Eh? We could go back to my flat. It's nice and cool up there. Only gets the sun in the mornings.

Rachel says nothing. She carries on cleaning the bath.

Sit on the bed. Watch a video. What d'yer think? Eh?

Rachel gets up. She still says nothing. She wipes the top of the bath. Sid gets up and stands by the bath, opposite her.

What's up? 'Ave I said somethin'? Eh?

RACHEL
(*shaking her head*)

No.

Sid walks out of the room. As he gets to the door, the large Care Worker rushes past. She spots Rachel, and reappears in the doorway. She is wearing rubber gloves.

CARE WORKER

Oh . . . Rachel, when you got a moment, you couldn't 'ave a look in Bertha's room – she's in the lounge now. Only she's managed to do a bit of a Number Two's on the carpet

again – I cleaned most of it up, it just needs a bit of a mop
'n' that – alright?

*She scuttles off. Rachel starts rinsing the bath with the shower. She
looks anxious.*

*Maureen is doing her ironing in her living room. She glances out of
the window at the weather. A sunny day.*

*Meanwhile, Carol, who is fairly drunk, is making her unsteady way
across the estate. She comes across Rory, who is idly kicking his ball.
He is alone. Carol stops.*

RORY

Alright?

Carol comes up close to him and strokes his hair.

CAROL

You're on your own, in't yer?

She strokes his face.

RORY

So?

Carol looks vague. Then she hobbles away. Rory watches her go.

*Phil is in his car on a suburban main road. The traffic isn't very
heavy. His rear-seat passenger is a smart French woman in
fashionable spectacles, and dressed in black. She is holding a large
antique Chinese vase, which is wrapped in newspaper. It will transpire
that she is called Cécile.*

CÉCILE

You are know the centre of London, the West End?

PHIL

Yeah.

CÉCILE

You 'ave been there?

PHIL

Oh, yeah.

CÉCILE

Ah, bon.

Pause. She drums on the vase with her fingers.

It will be much traffique?

PHIL

You might be lucky. 'Ave you got an appointment?

CÉCILE

Mais oui, I must go to the opera, *Don Giovanni* . . . It will
take 'ow long?

PHIL

Well . . . It's unpredictable, innit? You should be alright.

Cécile settles back in her seat.

The estate, on a walkway. Maureen is carrying some ironing. A young woman backs out of a flat with a little boy in a push-chair.

WOMAN
Come on . . . come on, babe. There you go.

MAUREEN
Alright, Michelle?

MICHELLE
Hello, Maureen.

Another young woman comes out of the flat, also with a little boy in a push-chair. Michelle goes to close her door.

MAUREEN
I've brought your little shirts.

Michelle takes them.

MICHELLE
Oh, right. I – I thought you was comin' after tea.

MAUREEN
Nah. (*She hands Michelle the rest of the shirts.*)

MICHELLE
Right . . . D'you want the money now?

MAUREEN
Yeah! It ain't free.

Michelle takes the garments inside.

Alright, Ange?

ANGE
Alright, Maureen? Not at work today?

MAUREEN
No, it's me day off . . . Doin' me ironin'. (*to one of the kids*)
Oi!

Phil's car enters the Blackwall Tunnel (which runs under the Thames). Now we are inside the tunnel . . .

CÉCILE

I do not like zis tunnel. Why you not tell me . . . 'We must make ze tunnel – do you wish another route?' You say nothing.

PHIL

Are you claustrophobic?

CÉCILE

You must say to the passenger, 'Excusez-moi, madame . . . we must make ze tunnel – it is okay?' C'est pas compliqué, comme même.

PHIL

Well, we're stuck in it now, I'm afraid.

CÉCILE

Evidemment, 'stuck on it'.

Pause. They progress through the tunnel.

PHIL

I walked through 'ere when I was a boy, once. South to North. Me and my best mate. My face turned completely black. 'E was already black. (*Pause.*) 'Ow d' you get on with the whatsit? – the . . . Channel Tunnel.

CÉCILE

Il insiste, quoi! I do not want to talk about ze Channel Tunnel, okay? – or any tunnel. Anyway, with the train it is complètement différent. You see nothing. Zis conversation is very boring for me.

PHIL

Fair enough.

CÉCILE

You are married?

PHIL

Yeah.

CÉCILE

With ze children?

PHIL

Yeah, I got two – a girl and a boy.

CÉCILE

Oh. Oh, mais c'est formidable.

They have emerged from the tunnel into the sunshine.

PHIL

Alright?

On the estate. As Michelle and Ange pass by with their boys, three youths are winding up Rory. They pass his ball between them, taunting him with provocative jibes. Rory is in a very agitated state.

RORY

Just fuckin' give it back . . .

He gets into a vicious if brief fight with one of the kids, while the other two pass the ball between them. The scrap ends and Rory moves away from his adversary. The others taunt him . . . .

FIRST YOUTH

Come on, fat boy!

SECOND YOUTH

Go on, fat boy – come and get your ball back, mate!

Rory suddenly clutches his chest, and loses interest in the others. He is panting heavily. They taunt him a bit more, then they run off. Carol appears in the distance. Maureen comes out of a flat on a walkway.

MAUREEN

See you, Deb.

DEB

(*unseen, from inside*)

Yeah – see you later, Maureen!

Deb closes her door. Maureen has obviously had a jolly few minutes with her – she is smiling. But as she stops and glances in Rory's direction, the smile fades. Rory is still clutching his chest. He is now coughing, and is bent over. Maureen takes a closer look. Rory now staggers forward. Maureen starts running along the walkway at great speed.

MAUREEN

Rory!!

Rory staggers on. His pain is obviously increasing by the moment, and he can hardly breathe. He collapses on the grass and rolls over into a sitting position, clutching his chest even more desperately. Carol comes towards him. She is carrying a blue plastic carrier bag. When she reaches him, she drops her shopping and half-bends down to him.

CAROL

Oh, sweet'eart . . . D'you wanna cry?

Maureen arrives. She has run across the grass.

MAUREEN

What's the matter with 'im?

She crouches down and puts her arm round Rory.

Rory!

RORY

Che– my chest . . .

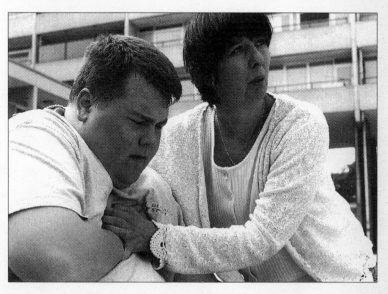

MAUREEN

You got pains? In your chest?

Rory nods. He can scarcely catch his breath now.

Get an ambulance, Carol.

CAROL

What?

MAUREEN

Go and phone for an ambulance.

Carol doesn't move.

I think 'e's 'avin' an 'eart attack.

CAROL

An 'eart attack? Is 'e?

MAUREEN

Yes!!!

Carol still doesn't move.

Carol – go on!!!

Carol hesitates, then goes.

D'you wanna lay down?

Carol scuttles back, grabs her shopping and goes. Maureen helps Rory to lie down. But as soon as he hits lying-down position, he gasps, and wants to sit up. Maureen helps him to do this. She looks towards Carol.

Where are you goin'?!!

Carol is going in the wrong direction. She stops, looks round, gets her bearings, and scuttles off in the right direction.

MAUREEN
(*quietly, to Rory*)

You'll be alright.

Rory lies down abruptly.

Oh! (*to herself*) Oh, fuck! (*shouting, to Carol*) Hurry up!! And phone Penny!!

CAROL
(*stopping*)

What?!

MAUREEN

Safeway!!

Carol takes this in with some difficulty, then scuttles off.

In Phil's car. Cécile is still his passenger.

PHIL

Yeah . . . She works in an old people's home. I'm proud of her.

CÉCILE

You're a very lucky man.

PHIL

We're all gonna die one day.

CÉCILE

Sans doute.

She examines her antique vase, and pats its newspaper wrapping.

PHIL

Was it a bargain?

CÉCILE

Of course. It is for my client in New York.

Pause. Phil nods, as if to say, 'I see'.

And your son? 'E work with you in the taxi?

PHIL

No, 'e don't do nothing.

CÉCILE

Comment cela?

PHIL

I beg your pardon?

CÉCILE

'Ow 'e don't do nothing?

PHIL

He does a lot of nothing.

CÉCILE

Eh?

PHIL

Mind you . . . if eatin' was an Olympic event, 'e'd be the
world champion by now.

CÉCILE
(*mirthlessly*)
Ah, it is a joke . . . It is very funny. 'E is fat, like you?

PHIL
(*amused*)
Yeah . . . 'e's a big boy, yeah . . . (*He chortles.*)

*In Ron and Carol's flat. Samantha comes out of the loo. She is
chewing gum. The front door is open.*

SAMANTHA
(*puzzled*)

Mum?

*Carol is standing, holding the telephone receiver. She is paralysed with
fear and inertia – and vodka.*

What's the matter?

Carol thrusts the receiver at her.

What?

CAROL

Gotta phone ambulance . . .

SAMANTHA

What's 'appened? Mum!!

CAROL

'Eart attack.

She indicates the front door.

SAMANTHA

'Oo's 'ad an 'eart attack?

She runs onto the walkway, takes one look at what's going on down on the grass, and gets it.

Fuck!!

She rushes back inside and pushes Carol out of the way.

Get out o' the fuckin' way!!

She grabs the receiver from Carol, and taps in the emergency number.

Come on . . .!

They reply.

Ambulance. Fuck's sake . . .

In Phil's car. We are now in the West End of London.

CECILE

Alors, er . . . I am there in the brasserie . . . I am very
'appy; I am dressed very nice, I am thinking, 'It is very
good, I will make the twenty-fiveth birthday with my son.
It will be good, we will make the good relationship . . . '
Eight o'clock, 'e is not there; eight-thirty; nine o'clock . . .
les garçons are looking at me – I am ashamed. 'Alf past
nine 'e arrive with the two girls with the red plastic dress like
zis – (*She demonstrates their bosoms.*) 'E say, 'Maman, I 'ave
already eat. We go now to the casino?' I say, 'No, Nicholas,
no – ça suffit . . . c'est fini.

PHIL

Shame.

Pause. Cécile looks out of the window.

CÉCILE

We are nearly there!

PHIL

About five minutes. (*Pause.*) What does your husband say?

CÉCILE

My husband?

PHIL

Yeah . . .

CÉCILE

'E don't say nothing. 'E is in Algeria. We are divorced.

PHIL
(*quietly*)

Oh.

*Pause. The car has been stationary for a while. Now it moves off
again.*

*Samantha rushes onto the balcony outside her flat. Maureen is still
down on the grass, nursing Rory. A small group of people has gathered
round them.*

SAMANTHA
(*shouting*)

Is 'e still breathing?

MAUREEN
(*shouting*)

Yes!!

*Samantha turns to run back into the flat. Carol is hovering in the
doorway. Samantha pushes her aside.*

SAMANTHA

Get out of the fuckin' way!! (*She picks up the receiver.*) Yeah,
'e's breathin' . . . (*Pause.*) Well, I dunno – if 'e's breathin',
'e's got a pulse, ain't 'e? (*Pause.*) I ain't with 'im – I ain't
there. I'm up 'ere – 'e's down there.

In Phil's car.

CÉCILE

You are caring for your wife?

PHIL

Pardon?

CÉCILE

Do you love your wife?

PHIL

Yeah. Oh, yeah . . . Funny, innit? Wossername? Love . . .
It's like a drippin' tap . . . Bucket's either 'alf-full . . . or it's
'alf-empty. If you're not together, you're alone. You're born
alone, you die alone. Nothing you can do about it.

CÉCILE

You are right – it is fuckin' lonely.

Pause. They both reflect on things.

*Carol is sitting in her living room, swigging from a half-bottle of
vodka. Samantha comes in from the walkway.*

SAMANTHA

Mum!

CAROL
(*to herself*)
Should've phoned Penny . . .

SAMANTHA
What?!

CAROL
Safeway.

SAMANTHA
For fuck's sake, Mum! You're a waste of space – you're disgustin'! I'll get the number.

She picks up the receiver. Carol has another swig.

Phil is parked in a busy street. He opens the rear passenger door and leans in.

PHIL
Alright?

CÉCILE
Oui, oui.

Phil picks up the vase, which is lying on the back seat.

Be careful.

PHIL
Yeah, got it.

CÉCILE
Alors, on y va.

She gets out of the car and mores off. Phil closes the car door and follows her. They are outside her hotel. Cécile stops on the steps and turns to Phil.

What is your name?

PHIL
Phil.

Phil?

Yeah.

I am Cécile. Bon.

Cécile turn, and enters the hotel. Phil follows. Inside, half-audible . . . .

Alors, c'est par là.

She indicates where she wants Phil to put the vase. The two of them disappear out of sight. We hold on the hotel exterior, looking at the empty foyer through the glass doors. Phil reappears and comes out. He stands on the steps for a moment, then gets into his car.

A few minutes later. Phil pulls up in a busy street nearby. He reflects for a little while. He is very agitated. He turns off his mini-cab walkie-talkie. Then he takes out his mobile and turns that off, too. And then he just sits there, thinking.

At Safeway. A Supervisor runs through the crowded store.

Penny! Penny . . .

Penny is at her till, processing shopping. The Supervisor leans across and speaks to her discreetly. At first Penny isn't interested and doesn't register what her colleague is saying. Then suddenly she hears the message. She jumps up. A look of horror and panic. Tears well up. The Supervisor takes over. Penny removes her spectacles and runs off through the store at great speed.

The estate. An aerial shot: a crowd watches as Rory, on a stretcher, is put by paramedics into the back of an ambulance.

The supermarket. Removing her uniform overall as she goes, Penny rushes into the women's staff changing room. She passes a middle-aged woman fellow-worker who says, 'Hi, Penny.' She opens her locker with the key, and takes out her coat.

At the estate, three lads on mountain bikes race after the ambulance as it speeds off with its siren blaring.

As Penny rushes out of the store, she overtakes a woman customer in the doorway.

PENNY

Mind out the way!

Carrying her coat and her crash helmet, and with her mobile to her ear, she runs at great speed to her bicycle, and starts to unlock it. But she has second thoughts, and doesn't bother. She is very upset. She speaks into her mobile.

Come on, Phil!

On a motorway, outside London. Phil is in his car. He is very intense.

Outside Safeway. Penny is on her mobile.

PENNY

Come on . . .

By the wide River Thames. Against the skyline of the Millennium Dome and cranes and high-rise development, Rachel strolls alone in the late afternoon sunlight.

In the hospital. Accompanied by doctors, nurses, paramedics and Maureen, Rory is rushed alone a corridor on a stretcher with wheels.

PARAMEDIC
You're nearly there now, mate.

In the High Dependency Unit. Rory is lifted onto a bed. Several nurses. Much bustle. Maureen watches.

NURSE
Okay, Rory, you're in good hands now – okay?

At the mini-cab office. Dinah picks up the phone.

DINAH
Gladiator Cars, Dinah speakin', how can I help?

At the supermarket. Penny is on her mobile. The rest of this scene intercuts between supermarket and cab office.

PENNY
'Ello – it's Penny. Phil's Penny – d'you know where 'e is?

DINAH
No.

NEVILLE
Who's that?

DINAH
Penny, Phil's wife.

NEVILLE
Give me the phone. (*He takes it.*) Hi, Penny, it's Neville – what's up?

PENNY
Yeah – I can't get 'old o' Phil.

NEVILLE
I know. 'E's gone off the air and 'e's switched off 'is phone. I don't know what 'e's playin' at.

PENNY

Yeah – well can you, can you send us a taxi up at Safeway's?
I got to get down the 'ospital – me son's been taken in.

NEVILLE

Er – no problem.

PENNY

Yeah, straightaway, an' – I'm, I'm waitin' outside the front
entrance.

NEVILLE

Yeah – you just wait there, yeah? I'll get someone out to
you.

PENNY

Yeah . . . yeah, ta. (*She terminates the conversation on her
mobile.*)

At the mini-cab office . . .

NEVILLE

She's at Safeway's – put a call out.

Dinah presses a button with her pen.

DINAH

Can anyone go Safeway's?

Pause. No reply. She presses the button again.

Is there anyone free for Safeway's?

Ron's voice is heard over the air . . . .

RON

Two-seven.

DINAH

Two-seven, can you pick up Penny, Phil's wife?

*Ron is in his parked car, reading a newspaper. He is wearing his
shades. During the following, we intercut.*

RON

Yes, I can do that.

DINAH

She's got to go to hospital.

RON

Is she alright?

NEVILLE

No, it's the son.

Dinah presses the button.

DINAH

Something wrong with the son.

RON

On me way.

He starts the car.

At the mini-cab office. Dinah is filing her nails. Neville is smoking a fag.

DINAH

Can I go home?

NEVILLE

Yeah. But I'm dockin' your wages.

Dinah stops filing her nails.

DINAH

I'm tellin' Mummy.

She resumes filing. Neville sucks his teeth.

Outside the supermarket. Ron speeds through the car park, blows his horn and screeches to a halt by Penny.

PENNY

Oh, 'ello, Ron.

'Ello, Penny.

Penny starts to get into the back of the car.

Oh – sorry!

She rushes round the car and gets into the front.

Sorry, I nearly got in the back there – I can't think straight.

She closes the door and the car takes off – at great speed.

In the hospital. Rory is in bed. He is very tired and docile. He wears no top, but he has two ECG pads attached to his chest, and a naso-gastric tube in his nose. A heart monitor is behind him. He is being attended to by a woman Nurse and a young Doctor with an open-neck shirt, a trendy stubble, spectacles and a Welsh accent. He is wearing a stethoscope. Maureen stands at the foot of the bed.

NURSE
Rory, we're gonna sit you up, okay? After three – one, two, three – up!

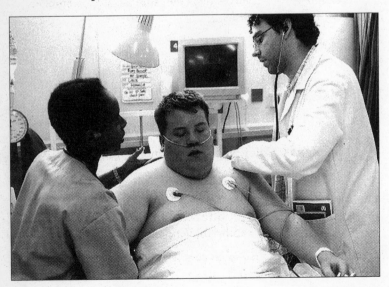

DOCTOR
(*joining in*)

Up!

They sit Rory up.

Now then, let's have a deep breath, Rory.

He puts his stethoscope to Rory's back. Rory takes a deep breath.

Good. And another one . . .

Rory breathes again.

Excellent – okay.

NURSE

Lie back.

They lie him down.

DOCTOR

Wicked! And another . . .

He puts his stethoscope to Rory's chest. Rory breathes.

Magic. And . . . one more. Sweet as a nut. Normal breathin' now. So you're not quite sure if you're a smoker, then, Rory! (*He chortles.*)

Rory doesn't say anything.

MAUREEN
(*jolly*)
'T's alright – I won't tell your mum!

DOCTOR
(*amused*)
What d'you 'ave for breakfast this morning, Rory?

RORY
Er . . . fried-egg sandwich.

DOCTOR
Ooh . . . fried-egg sandwich! Very tasty!

He takes his stethoscope out of his ears. Maureen is laughing.

Penny and Ron are travelling in Ron's car.

RON

Course, you can 'ave an 'eart attack without knowing about it.

PENNY

Can yer?

RON

Yeah, you just don't feel very well – Christ, there's some arseholes on the road!!

He overtakes an ice-cream van just as a car backs out in front of him. He crashes straight into its side. Penny looks ahead, in horror.

RON

Fuck!!! (*He gets out of the car and rushes over to the other driver.*) Dickhead!! You fuckin' dickhead!!

The other driver, a guy in his thirties, gets out of his car.

What the fuck were you doin'?!!

Ron is in a total rage. He examines the damage. Smoke is pouring from under his bonnet.

Oh, for fuck's sake!!!

Penny gets out of the car.

OTHER DRIVER

I didn't see you coming round the van.

RON

You didn't fuckin' look, did you?!

Penny hesitates, then takes off, and runs away at great speed from the mayhem of the accident. She still carries her rucksack and her crash helmet. She is crying.

In the hospital. Maureen is sitting by Rory's bed.

MAUREEN

You alright, Rory? D'you want another drink?

                    RORY
                  (*faintly*)
    Yeah . . .

*Maureen gets up. She is holding a glass of water. She puts her hand
gently behind Rory's head and raises it a little. He drinks.*

                    MAUREEN
    Not too quick . . .

*Penny rushes into the hospital and along the busy Accident and
Emergency corridor . . .*

*Now she enters the ante-room outside Rory's ward. Maureen looks up.
She can see Maureen through the semi-frosted window. Penny sees
her and rushes in.*

                    PENNY
                  (*crying*)
    Rory!!

*She dashes to the bedside. She takes Rory's hand. He tries to lean
towards her. She hugs him. Maureen moves away. Penny puts her
crash helmet on the bed between Rory's legs. Maureen discreetly moves
it to a table. Penny and Rory hug each other emotionally.*

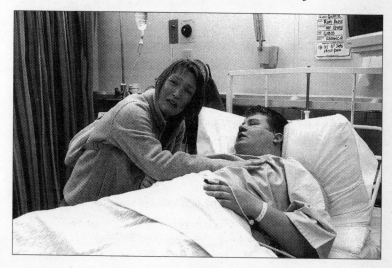

What's 'appened to you, Rory? (*She stands up.*) What's this?
'E's got tubes comin' out of 'im all over . . .

She notices Maureen.

What're you doin' 'ere, Maureen?

MAUREEN
I come with 'im in the ambulance.

PENNY
Oh, did yer? What 'appened, Rory?

RORY
(*hardly audible*)
I couldn't breathe.

MAUREEN
'E 'ad pains . . . in the chest.

PENNY
(*to Rory*)
Don't worry . . . I'll look after you. (*in tears, to Maureen*)
This is my little baby boy.

*She kisses Rory. Maureen looks at them. A wide range of emotions.
Then she quietly leaves the ward, and leans against a wall in the ante-
room with her back to the world. Penny kisses Rory. They are both still
crying.*

RORY
Where's Dad?

PENNY
Yeah . . . 'e'll be 'ere in a bit.

*She looks round at Maureen, whom she can see through the window.
Then she looks at Rory's monitor.*

*A spacious, flat coastal place. A vast, blue sky, graced by a few placid
clouds. A lighthouse and a strange, tall wooden structure dominate the
landscape. Two small black shacks squat by a roadside. Wild yellow
grass, dotted with spiky black plants. Nobody around, except for a*

couple of tiny figures walking on the distant horizon. Phil's car moves into view. It slows down by the shacks, and turns a corner. It carries on for a little while. Then it comes to a halt. Nothing happens. Phil sits in his car. We can hear the sea.

Penny and Maureen are sitting either side of Rory's bed, facing each other. Rory is asleep.

MAUREEN

She was pissed as a fart. Good job Samantha was in.

PENNY

Yeah . . . yeah, well, thanks anyway, Maureen.

MAUREEN

'T's alright. (*Pause.*) I'm starvin'. I was just gonna make meself a bit of cheese-on-toast. Are you 'ungry?

PENNY

No.

MAUREEN

When's your Phil and Rachel comin' up?

PENNY

Well, Rachel ain't at 'ome. She's probably gone up the market or some'ing. I'll try and give 'er another ring in a minute.

MAUREEN

My Donna ain't in, either.

PENNY
(*whispering*)

I can't get 'old of Phil.

MAUREEN

Why, where is 'e?

Penny puts a 'shush' finger to her lips.

119

Phil plods along an empty pebble beach. He passes a few ancient sheds and a decaying fishing boat. Then he is gone.

Now he stands on the beach by the waves, looking out to sea. A ship moves slowly across the distant horizon. The wind blows Phil's hair. He reflects on things for a while. Then he moves on.

At the hospital. Penny is sitting in the corridor outside Rory's ward. She has her mobile to her ear. Rachel appears beside her.

RACHEL

Mum.

PENNY
(*looking up*)

Oh . . . hello, Rache. (*She stands up.*) I'm just tryin' to get 'old of your dad – I don't know what's 'appened to 'im.

Rachel touches Penny comfortingly. Penny sobs.

D'you get the bus alright?

RACHEL

Yeah.

Pause.

PENNY

'E's in 'ere.

She leads the way to the door into the ward. At this moment the Doctor who examined Rory earlier arrives. He holds the door for Penny and Rachel.

DOCTOR
(*cheerful*)

Sorry – after you. There you go.

They all go in.

In the ward.

PENNY
(*to the Nurse*)

It's 'is sister.

NURSE
(*to Rachel*)

Hi.

PENNY

Rory . . . Rachel's come to see you.

Rachel and Penny stand either side of the bed. Rory turns his head to Rachel. The Doctor signals to the Nurse, who draws the curtain round the bed. Then she leaves.

DOCTOR

Rory's mum?

PENNY

Yeah.

DOCTOR

Hi – I'm Simon Griffiths. I'm the doctor. I examined Rory before tea. And I bet you're Rory's sister!

RACHEL

Yeah.

DOCTOR

Hi. Hello, Rory. So . . . why don't we 'ave a sit-down, and we can 'ave a bit of a chat, okay? Make yourselves at home. Get comfy.

They all sit, Penny and Rachel on chairs either side of the bed, the Doctor on the bed next to Penny.

PENNY

Is 'e gonna be alright?

DOCTOR

Yeah, 'e's gonna be fine. We've run some tests – X-ray, checked 'is blood, etcetera –

PENNY

Ain't 'e 'ad a 'eart attack?

DOCTOR

Well, yes and no.

PENNY

What d'you mean?

DOCTOR

He's had a kind of heart attack. You see, in your heart, you've got four chambers, divided by a big wall of muscle, okay? And Rory's got a problem with this muscle.

He demonstrates this by drawing an imaginary diagram on his shirt.

PENNY

But 'e ain't never 'ad nothing like that before.

DOCTOR

Well, that's the thing, you see. 'E's probably 'ad it since 'e was a baby, but it's only just come to light.

PENNY

I can't believe all this.

DOCTOR

Yeah, I know. We think that's what must be wrong with Rory. But the consultant's got to 'ave a look at 'im tomorrow.

PENNY

What's gonna 'appen?

DOCTOR

Well, good news is, 'e should be 'ome within a week. But the thing with this condition is that it won't just go away, and we can't actually cure it, as such.

PENNY
(*sobbing*)

Can't yer?!

DOCTOR

No, 'fraid not. We're goin' to 'ave to put Rory on medication.

PENNY

'Ow long for?

DOCTOR

Er, probably for the rest of his life.

PENNY
(*fraught*)
Oh, no – that don't seem right!!

DOCTOR
Not to worry – lots of people take pills every day of their lives, and they're none the worse for it. Okay, Rory'll pop in, see a cardiologist every six months, and everything should be . . . cool.

Penny sobs.

'E's through the worst of it now.

PENNY
'E's only little.

DOCTOR
(*amused*)
'E's been a good lad.

PENNY
Yeah, he is a good lad.

DOCTOR
Does 'e smoke?

PENNY
No.

RACHEL
Yeah, 'e does a bit.

RORY
(*under his breath*)
Fuck off!

PENNY
Rory! Sorry, doctor. Rory!

DOCTOR
(*very amused*)
Well, once Rory's decided whether 'e smokes or not, then 'e can give it up. The same goes for burgers and chips and fry-ups and crisps – all that crap, eh, Rory? The sooner you get rid o' them, the better it'll be for you.

Penny and Rachel are embarrassed.

Dusk. Phil is in his car on a busy main road. His mobile rings. He picks it up, looks at it, and answers it.

PHIL

Hello?

PENNY'S VOICE

Phil, it's me. Where the bloody 'ell 'ave you been?

PHIL

What's up?

Penny is on an outdoor balcony at the hospital. During the following, we intercut between her and the car.

PENNY

I've been tryin' to get 'old of you since five o'clock this afternoon. Your phone's off, your radio's off, Neville can't get 'old of you, nobody can get 'old of you, what's goin' on? Where are you?

PHIL

I'm – I'm on the A2.

PENNY

Rory's 'ad a 'eart attack.

Phil doesn't respond.

Phil!!

PHIL

What?

PENNY

We're up at the 'ospital – South London General.

PHIL

Wh . . . what d'you mean, 'eart attack?

PENNY

What d'you mean, what do I mean, 'eart attack?

PHIL

Is 'e alright?

PENNY

No, 'e ain't alright!!

PHIL

'E ain't dead, is 'e?

PENNY

Of course 'e ain't dead! Where are you?

PHIL

Well . . . I'm just coming to that . . . big Chinese supermarket – you know, the one on the roundabout, down by the –

PENNY
(*covering her mouth*)
Phil – for fuck's sake!! Just 'urry up and get 'ere, alright?!

She turn off her phone, and walks away.

PHIL

Pen? Hello?

He puts down his phone, and keeps driving. He looks desperate.

In the hospital. Rachel sits and watches Rory as he sleeps.

Maureen and Donna are sitting in their living room. Maureen has a plate of toast on her lap.

MAUREEN

It's funny, I'm starvin', but . . . I can't eat this. Got a bleedin' 'eadache. D'you wanna bit?

DONNA

No, ta.

Maureen puts down the plate. Somewhere in a nearby flat, a baby starts to cry.

Is 'e gonna be alright?

Yeah. 'E's in good 'ands. 'Ear that baby?

DONNA

Yeah . . .

Pause. They both listen to the baby. Donna is anxious. She looks at Maureen. The baby stops crying.

MAUREEN

Look at you.

Donna's eyes fill with tears.

Come 'ere (*She gets up.*) Shift up.

She sits with Donna on the sofa, and puts her arms round her. Donna rests her head on Maureen's shoulder. Pause.

Are you scared?

Donna nods.

We'll be alright. (*Pause.*) 'Ere . . . what if it's a boy?

They both reflect on this prospect.

In Carol's and Ron's bedroom. Ron lies on the bed, half-sitting up. Carol strokes his hair. Both are drunk and fully clothed.

CAROL

Just forget about it.

RON

'Ow can I forget about it? I'll fuckin' kill 'im.

CAROL
(*sympathetic*)

Yeah . . .

Samantha appears in the doorway.

SAMANTHA

Are you goin' to phone the police, Dad?

RON

No.

SAMANTHA

Why not?

RON

I'll do it in the mornin'.

SAMANTHA

Do it now.

RON

No!

SAMANTHA

I'll phone 'em.

CAROL

Leave it.

SAMANTHA

Give us that bit of paper.

She comes to the bed and holds out her hand. No response.

Dad!

Pause.

RON

What?!

SAMANTHA

That bloke's gonna get away with it, in 'e?

CAROL

It's none of your fuckin' business!

SAMANTHA

(to Carol)

'Ave you phoned Penny yet? You ain't, ave yer? You don't give a shit, do yer? You're useless. You're both fuckin' useless. I'm goin' out.

She walks out of the room. We hear her going down the stairs. Carol continues to stroke Ron's hair. Then he collapses back on the bed. Carol surveys him through her alcoholic haze.

Now Samantha walks alone, somewhere on the estate. She is chewing gum. Suddenly, out of the darkness, Craig comes, rushing towards her, panting and agitated. He stops a little distance away from her, under some trees. She stops.

SAMANTHA

What?

He zips open his tracksuit top and pulls back his shirt to reveal his chest. He has carved a letter 'S' into his bare flesh.

Oh, God!

She is immediately distressed, and becomes tearful. She turns and walks away.

Oh, fuckin' 'ell, what you done?

She walks round a tree. He smiles. She comes back to him and looks closely at the wound.

Why d'you do that, eh?

CRAIG

It's alright. I love you, an 'all.

SAMANTHA
I don't love you, alright? I don't even like yer. You need to get that seen to – you need to go to hospital, alright?

Craig laughs – in joy at her concern.

It's not funny. It's not funny!

He laughs again. Samantha sobs.

I'm sorry.

She strokes his hair.

I'm sorry.

She puts her arms round him and hugs him and sobs deeply. His smile is ecstatic. Then she turns and walks away from him quickly. He watches her disappear into the night.

In her bedroom, Samantha sits up in bed in her pyjamas. She sobs her heart out.

In the hospital. Phil approaches the semi-frosted window in Rory's ward. He looks through it, and sees Penny and Rachel, still on either side of Rory's bed. Penny and Rory are asleep. The Nurse approaches Phil.

NURSE

Excuse me.

Phil turns to her.

Can I help you?

PHIL

That's my boy.

NURSE

Can you tell me his name, please?

PHIL

Rory Bassett.

NURSE

Okay, Mr Bassett, in you go. (*She walks away.*)

PHIL

Right.

NURSE
(*calling*)

It's only two by a bedside.

PHIL

Okay. Sorry.

He looks through the window at his family again, then proceeds very cautiously to the door. He opens it and stands in the doorway. Penny wakes up and looks at him.

PENNY

It's only two allowed by the bed.

PHIL

Yeah . . . I'll wait outside, then.

PENNY

Don't be stupid – you've only just got 'ere.

RACHEL

Oh, no – it's alright. (*She gets up.*)

PENNY

Get yourself a cuppa tea.

RACHEL

I'll just wait outside.

She goes to the door and stops by Phil.

PHIL

Alright?

RACHEL

Yeah.

She goes out. Phil closes the door, looks round the ward, and goes to the empty side of the bed.

PENNY

He's asleep now.

PHIL

Is 'e?

He looks at Rory and at all the medical paraphernalia around him.

'As 'e 'ad an operation?

> PENNY

No.

Pause.

> PHIL

I got lost . . . downstairs. A bloke said, 'Go upstairs –'

> PENNY

Yeah, alright, Phil – you're 'ere now, ain't yer?

Pause.

> PHIL

What happened?

> PENNY

Well, 'e collapsed. Maureen was with 'im when I come up 'ere. 'E's gotta take pills for the rest of 'is life.

> PHIL

You never know what's gonna 'appen, do you? (*He sits.*)
It's wossername, a fait accompli. He might win the Lottery tomorrow. It's kismet, innit?

> PENNY

What're you talkin' about? Where 'ave you been?

> PHIL

Out and about, I . . . y'know.

> PENNY

Where?

> PHIL

Been a . . . long run . . . down . . .

> PENNY

You're supposed to be a taxi, Phil. What are you doin' with your radio switched off, and your mobile? What's the point of 'avin' them if we can't get 'old of you when we need you?

PHIL

Yeah, I know what you mean.

PENNY

It's pathetic!

Pause.

RORY
(*quietly*)

Leave it out, Mum.

Penny looks at him, startled.

Stop 'avin' a go at 'im.

PENNY

Rory! I ain't 'avin' a go at 'im. (*She breaks down and cries.*)

PHIL

'T's alright.

Rory turns towards Phil.

RORY

Alright, Dad?

Phil gets up and leans over him.

PHIL

Alright, mate? You've been in the wars, ain't yer?

He strokes Rory's shoulder.

D'you wanna go on 'oliday?

Penny looks at him.

PENNY

What?

PHIL

We'll all go away. When 'e's better. Yeah, four of us? Yeah?
Disneyworld?

Penny is gazing at Phil incredulously. He looks at her.

What?

Penny looks at Rory. She is nonplussed.

In the empty corridor outside the ward. Rachel sits alone, holding her coat.

In the ward, the Nurse approaches the bed.

NURSE

It is past ten o'clock.

PENNY

I don't wanna leave 'im.

NURSE

I know. But the night staff will take good care of him. Okay?

She leaves them. Phil and Penny get up. Penny leans close to Rory.

PENNY

Rory . . . gotta go 'ome now. Be back in the mornin'.

RORY

Alright.

PHIL

Alright, mate?

Penny kisses Rory on the cheek.

PENNY

I love you, Rory.

Phil watches them.

In the corridor. A male nurse passes Rachel. Penny comes out of the ward, putting on her coat. Phil follows.

Rachel gets up.

PENNY

Got to go 'ome now.

RACHEL

Is 'e asleep?

PENNY

Yeah. Nearly.

PHIL

'E'll be alright.

Penny sets off down the long, empty corridor. Phil and Rachel follow. Phil puts his arm round Penny, but after a few moments she detaches herself.

In Phil's car. The three of them travel in silence. Rachel sits at the rear.

In the flat. Phil hangs up his coat in the hall. He and Penny come into the unlit living room. For a moment they stand together in the darkness. Then Penny goes into the kitchen, where Rachel is standing. She has put on the kitchen light.

PENNY

Makin' a cuppa tea?

RACHEL

Yeah. D'you want one?

PENNY

No, I'll 'ave a 'ot chocolate.

Phil has followed Penny into the kitchen. He opens the fridge.

PHIL

D'you wanna beer?

PENNY

No.

Phil takes out a can of beer, and returns to the living room, where he puts on a light and sits in his armchair. Penny drifts back into the back part of the living room where the table is. She stands forlornly. The camera pans slowly to Phil, who is sitting holding his beer – forlornly.

A few minutes later. Rachel has sat on the sofa. Penny is leaning in a doorway.

PENNY

I wish I could've stayed the night up there with 'im.

PHIL

Yeah. Well, they'd 'ave drugged 'im up, knocked 'im out till mornin'. Wouldn't they, Rache?

RACHEL

Yeah.

PHIL

First thing, then . . . run you up there . . .

PENNY

No, you don't 'ave to do that.

PHIL

No, it's alright – I won't 'ang about. I'll come in with you, say 'ello, make sure 'e's alright, an' then get straight on the

136

radio . . . start work, soon as I can. 'E'll be surprised, won't
'e, Neville? 'E's a bit – wossername – unpredictable, in' 'e?
'E might not 'ave me. There's . . . lot o' blokes work
mornings regular. I might pick up some airport runs. If he
says no, I'll try somewhere else – I don't care.

PENNY

Yeah, I don't wanna talk about it now, Phil. (*She sits at the
table.*)

PHIL

No, I mean it. I'm gonna do it. I'm determined to do it.
Got to get started, get savin'. Shouldn't take long. I'll work
seven days a week. Start early; finish late; do nights,
weekends . . .

PENNY

Phil! Rory is in 'ospital!

PHIL

Yeah. Sorry. But I made 'im a promise. And I'm gonna
keep it.

PENNY

What promise?

PHIL

'Bout goin' on 'oliday.

PENNY

Phil!

PHIL

They do these deals, don't they? Disneyworld. These two
nurses I picked up was tellin' me about it. They do these
all-in packages . . . er, wossername – fly-drive. Florida, innit?

PENNY

Phil, it ain't about goin' on 'oliday. It's about gettin' by,
week in, week out. It ain't a game. (*Pause.*) Just 'cos you've
suddenly got some bee in your bonnet about gettin' up in
the mornings and goin' to work – when you've been lying
in bed for years, till God knows what time. And we're all

supposed to be grateful 'cos you've decided to do what normal people do – I get up in the mornings. Rachel gets up in the mornings. You make me sick. (*Pause.*) Doctor was askin' about you. About your 'eart an' stuff – your family. If anyone in your family's 'ad an 'eart attack. There was your Uncle Duggie, weren't there?

PHIL
(*quietly*)

Me nan 'ad one, an' all.

PENNY

Oh . . . yeah.

PHIL

Me mum's mum.

PENNY

I forgot about that.

PHIL

Me dad's eldest brother . . . whatsisname . . . in Australia.

PENNY

There you are, then. It's all on your side, innit? Ain't none on mine. (*Pause.*) Are you goin' to work in the mornin', Rache? Don't 'ave to – you can phone in.

RACHEL

I dunno.

PENNY

I ain't goin'.

PHIL

If you do, when you've done, give us a bell on me mobile. Run you up to the 'ospital, see your brother, yeah?

Rachel nods.

PENNY

Oh, you'll 'ave it switched on then, will yer? Not like today – your son's in 'ospital 'avin' a 'eart attack and we can't get 'old of you – they can get 'old of me; they know where I am in an emergency. But we can't get 'old of 'is dad, nowhere. (*Pause.*) Where was you, anyway? What you been doin' all day?

PHIL

I switched it off.

PENNY

Yeah, I know you switched it off. Why d'you switch it off?

PHIL

I'd 'ad enough.

PENNY

You'd 'ad enough? 'Ad enough o' what? 'Ad enough of workin' for five minutes, so you switched it off? What can I switch off when I've 'ad enough? 'Ad enough of gettin' up every mornin', goin' to work, doin' the shoppin', comin' 'ome, cookin' the tea, cleanin' the 'ouse, doin' the ironin', makin' sure everyone's got clean clothes on their back . . .

Rachel has got up, and leaves the room.

What can I switch off when I've 'ad enough? 'Ad enough of what, anyway?

PHIL

Everything.

PENNY

What? What everything?

Phil doesn't reply.

Pause.

For God's sake, Phil.

Pause.

PHIL

You don't love me no more, do you?

PENNY

What?

PHIL

You don't love me.

PENNY

Phil, what are you talkin' about? What's that got to do with
anything?

PHIL

It's . . . it's got to do with everything.

He turns round to look at her. He has tears in his eyes.

PENNY

Rory . . . 'as 'ad a 'eart attack.

Phil continues to look straight at Penny.

PHIL

You ain't loved me for years. You don't like me; you don't
respect me; you talk to me like I'm a piece of shit.

Penny's eyes fill with tears.

PENNY

I don't . . .

PHIL

You do.

PENNY

I, I don't, Phil – I don't talk to you like you're a piece of
shit.

PHIL

You do, Pen. You don't know you're doin' it, but you do.

PENNY
(*crying*)

That's stupid. That ain't fair. Why are you sayin' all this to
me?

PHIL

It's . . . it's, wossername . . . unbearable.

PENNY

What, what's unbearable?

You don't love me no more. Do you? Do you love me?
I gotta know.

Penny can't find what to say. Then:

PENNY
(*half-says*)

Well . . .

She weeps. Phil sobs.

PHIL
(*choking*)

If you don't love me no more, I might as well go.

PENNY

Go? Where you gonna go?

PHIL

I don't know. (*sobbing*) If I'm, if I'm makin' you un'appy –
you know what I mean . . . I ain't got no skills. I don't earn
enough money. I know I'm a disappointment to you – I know
I get on your nerves. It's like . . . like something's died. I feel
like an old tree that ain't got no water!!

They both sob.

When we first met, I couldn't believe it. A pretty girl like you,
goin' with a fat bloke like me. People lookin' at us. I felt,
I felt like the bee's knees. We ain't got much . . . but we got
each other . . . and that's enough. But if you don't want me,
we ain't got nothing. We ain't a family. And that's it.

*He sobs. Tears stream down Penny's face. Long pause. Then Penny gets
up and stands near Phil, who is still crying.*

Sorry . . . I know it ain't very 'elpful . . . what with Rory 'n'
that. I couldn't 'old it in.

PENNY

I don't talk to you like that, Phil.

PHIL

That's what it feels like.

He wipes his eyes on his shirt cuff.

PENNY

D'you want a tissue? I've got some.

PHIL

Yeah. Me shirt's all wet.

Penny goes out of the room.

In the hall, she takes a small packet of tissues out of her bag. Then she goes to the bottom of the stairs and calls up –

PENNY

Rachel!

But Rachel is sitting, huddled up, at the top of the stairs.

What're you doing there?

Rachel doesn't reply.

Penny starts to climb the stairs. Rachel scuttles away.

Rache!

Penny continues up the stairs.

In the living room, Phil wipes his eyes again.

Rachel's bedroom. Rachel is sitting on the bed. She has also been crying. Penny sits next to her. Pause. Then Penny puts her arms round her and cuddles her. Somewhere a motor horn sounds. The embrace ends. Penny gently tidies Rachel's hair away from her face.

RACHEL

You do talk to 'im like that.

PENNY

Do I?

RACHEL

Sometimes.

Penny kisses Rachel's forehead. Then she starts to get up. She stops, looks at Rachel, hesitates, and then leaves. Rachel sighs.

Penny comes down the stairs. She stops near the bottom, and reflects.

Phil is still sitting in the armchair.

Penny walks slowly into the room. She stops by him.

The following scene takes its time. The camera starts on a long shot and tracks very slowly into a tight close-up of Penny and Phil.

PHIL

Is she alright?

PENNY

Yeah . . .

PHIL

What did she say?

Pause.

PENNY

She – she's just a bit upset, that's all.

PHIL

Yeah.

Penny starts to take the packet of tissues out of her pocket.

PENNY

D'you – d'you want one of these?

PHIL

No, I'm . . . alright, thanks.

Penny doesn't take out the tissues. She looks at Phil for a few moments. Then she reaches down.

What?

She takes his hand.

Oh.

She kneels by him, holding his hand.

PENNY

Strange, isn't it?

PHIL

What?

PENNY

I dunno. I feel cut off all the time. Lonely . . .

PHIL

Yeah . . . me an' all.

PENNY

Do you?

Pause.

PHIL

I love you.

She cradles his hand in both her own hands. Then she kisses it. He strokes her face. He leans forward. They embrace and hold each other tight. They both sigh emotionally. They kiss lovingly. Then they press their noses together.

> PENNY

You used to make me laugh.

> PHIL

Yeah.

They smile. Then Phil puffs up his cheeks, and Penny 'bursts' them. They laugh. They caress each other.

D'you wanna go to bed?

> PENNY

Yeah. Busy day tomorrow.

Fade to blackout. The screen is blank for a few seconds.

The hospital. A sunny day. Phil, Penny and Rachel turn onto a busy corridor.

> PENNY

Oh, yeah – must be up 'ere.

> PHIL

Yeah.

Penny is wearing make-up. She is holding a carrier bag. Phil has shaved, and is carrying a bunch of bananas. Rachel walks behind them. They proceed along the corridor.

> PHIL

That's it.

> PENNY

Oh, yeah.

They look into a ward.

Oh, yeah, there 'e is.

PHIL

There 'e is.

As they go into the ward, Penny turns to Phil. She smiles.

PENNY

That's nice, by the window.

They walk down the ward. Rory is indeed in a bed by the window.
It is a big window, with a pleasant view of rooftops and trees.

You alright?

She kisses Rory on the cheek.

PHIL
(*quietly*)

Alright?

RORY

Alright?

Phil looks round the ward.

PHIL

There's no chairs.

Penny has a look.

PENNY

Yeah. Um . . . there's a couple over there.

PHIL

Oh, yeah.

He goes to get the chairs. Rachel moves round to the other side of the
bed, and sits with her back to the window. Penny takes off her coat.

PENNY

Are you alright there, Rache?

RACHEL

Yeah.

Phil brings two plastic stacking-chairs and puts them together by the
bed, facing Rachel.

PENNY
(*quietly, to Phil*)

Yeah . . . thanks.

Penny drapes her rucksack and her coat over the back of her chair.
She and Phil sit down. She smiles.

'E looks better, don't 'e? Got a bit of colour in 'is cheeks.

PHIL

Yeah.

PENNY

Ow'd they get you up 'ere?

RORY

I come up in a wheelchair.

PENNY

Did yer?

RORY

Yeah.

PHIL

Got you some bananas, mate.

RORY

Cheers.

The bananas are on the table.

PENNY

'Ere, I got you something, an' all.

RORY

Yeah, what is it?

Penny hands him the carrier bag.

PENNY

Well, open it.

Rory takes out some blue towelling.

RORY

What is it, a towel?

PENNY

No, it's a dressing gown.

RORY

Dressing gown? What do I need a dressing gown for?

PENNY

Yeah, for when you go toilet an' that.

RORY

Alright, well – stick it in there.

Penny takes it. Rory looks in the bag.

What's this, slippers?

PENNY

Yeah.

Rory takes out a pair of suede slippers.

RORY
(*enthusiastically*)

Cheers.

PHIL

They're moccasins, ain't they?

RORY

Yeah – nice one.

Rachel observes the slippers. Penny puts them away.

PENNY

They'll sort you out. You 'ad something to eat?

RORY

Yeah, I 'ad fish.

PENNY
(*amazed*)

Did you?!

PHIL

Nah!

RORY

Yeah.

PHIL

What, in batter?

RORY

No . . . with like . . . sauce on the top. Like, cheese.

PENNY

Cor blimey!

PHIL

D'you eat it?

RORY

Yeah.

PHIL

What, they tie you down, did they?

Rachel smiles.

RORY

No, it was nice. I 'ad that . . . and mash, and, like . . . green
. . . cauliflower stuff.

PENNY

Oh, yeah – broccoli.

RORY

I dunno. I ate it all.

PENNY

That's good.

PHIL

Blimey.

Rory turns to Rachel.

RORY

Are you alright?

RACHEL

Yeah.

PENNY

She ain't been back to work yet.

RACHEL

Yeah, I'm gonna go back tomorrow.

RORY

Why ain't you been in?

RACHEL

Well, I ain't been sleepin'.

RORY

Why not?

Pause. Rachel doesn't reply.

PENNY

She's been worried.

RORY

What about?

PENNY

About you. We all 'ave.

RORY

Shu' up. I'm alright.

PENNY

Yeah, you are now.

Pause.

PHIL
(*to Penny*)
You've got a bit of fluff on you . . .

PENNY

Oh – (*She giggles.*)

Phil flicks the fluff from her shoulder and then pretends to blow it away. They both smile – a loving moment. Rachel and Rory watch them.

PHIL

Did an airport this morning.

PENNY

Yeah – five o'clock!

RORY

Bloody 'ell.

PHIL

Yeah. Took this family to Gatwick. They was goin' to . . . wossername, Cyprus. Yeah, this bloke, two little boys, an' an old woman. Yeah . . . we was goin' along . . . and the kids started giggling, yeah. And, and the littlest one says, ''Ere, Dad . . . she's farted.'

Rory roars with laughter.

PENNY
(*smiling*)
'Ere, don't make 'im laugh! Are you 'urtin'?

151

PHIL
(*chuckling*)

'E's alright.

Rory is still amused.

Any'ow, so 'e turns round . . . 'e starts clumpin' em, says (*cod Greek Cypriot accent*) 'Don't be rude about your grandma!' 'E's swearin' in Greek, an' that.

Rory chuckles again.

I 'ad to open a window – it's . . . nah . . . it's –

He shakes his hand – a bad-smell-dispelling gesture. Rory's mirth erupts again.

PENNY
(*smiling*)

'Ad all sorts in that car!

PHIL
(*laughing*)

'T's right, yeah . . .

PENNY

You alright, Rache?

Rachel isn't smiling.

RACHEL

Yeah.

Rory has another burst of the giggles. Phil laughs with him.

PENNY
(*to Rory*)

You wanna be careful, you!

She looks at him. Then she looks at Phil. Phil smiles at her. They share a moment. Then Penny looks at Rachel . . . She has all sorts of thoughts and feelings and emotions. And she reflects on her lot.

We cut to a long shot, from the other end of the ward. Their conversation continues. We half-hear it.

PHIL

Got talkin' to anyone in 'ere?

RORY

No, I ain't.

PENNY

You've just got up 'ere, ain't you?

RORY

Yeah, I ain't spoken to no one.

PHIL

D'you get a card from your nan?

RORY

Yeah, it's that one there, yeah.

PENNY

Oh . . .

She picks up a greetings card from the bedside cupboard, and she shows it to Phil.

And there we leave them.